MW01639693

Keeping Your Family Close
When Frequent Travel Pulls You Apart

Keeping Your Family Close

When Frequent Travel Pulls You Apart

ELIZABETH M. HOEKSTRA

CROSSWAY BOOKS • WHEATON, ILLINOIS
A DIVISION OF GOOD NEWS PUBLISHERS

Keeping Your Family Close When Frequent Travel Pulls You Apart

Published by Crossway Books
a division of Good News Publishers
1300 Crescent Street
Wheaton, Illinois 60187

Cover design and photo: PAZ Design Group

First printing 1998

Printed in the United States of America

ISBN 1-56865-810-9

Contents

To Mom and Dad Marriner and Mom and Dad Hoekstra
for modeling love and lifelong commitment
in their Christian walks and marriages

Foreword

If you, like me, travel a lot for ministry or business purposes, you are going to find much help in *Keeping Your Family Close When Frequent Travel Pulls You Apart*. Men, you may not even realize what your wife is going through, what emotions she feels, because she is often trying to protect you. Because of the transparency in this book, you will find yourself quickly relating to the difficulties and challenges the author and her husband, Peter, experience in their marriage relationship resulting from his travel.

God has allowed me to minister to thousands nationally and internationally over the past thirty-five years. This has involved a lot of travel. But God has also given me a family, and they have expectations of me as husband and father. Elizabeth Hoekstra helps identify these kinds of expectations for us and shows us how to deal with them.

Like many husbands and fathers who travel a lot, I have lonely days, times when I ache to hold my family in my arms. This book shows how men who travel can deal with the loneliness—and how the wife can really help with that.

I know Dottie and the kids miss me a lot—and again Elizabeth Hoekstra shows how we as husbands and fathers can let our families know how much we love and care for them.

What we can learn, and what I am happy to see highlighted in *Keeping Your Family Close,* is the importance of communicating our feelings, especially our expectations of one another—and how we can make the most of our times together. We who travel often don't have the luxury of a lot of uninterrupted time with one another, so Dottie and I have learned how to communicate with greater openness and precision—much the same as Elizabeth Hoekstra recommends in this book.

I see this book not only as an excellent resource to which readers can return time and again, but also as a form of accountability in maintaining a God-honoring marriage. You, the reader, can find real help here if you are away from home only occasionally, as some are, or frequently, as I am.

—Josh McDowell

Acknowledgments

Even as the ink dried on the contract with Crossway Books for the publication of *Keeping Your Family Close*, Peter was on a business trip in Geneva, Switzerland. In his absence my time alone became one of those weeks when not just *something* went wrong, but *everything* seemed to go wrong. I felt overwhelmed with single-handedly meeting the needs of our ten animals and two children. I had work deadlines ominously marked in red on my calendar. Our daughter Geneva (yes, named after Geneva, Switzerland) became ill. One of the dogs developed an infection, and as if that weren't enough, my computer crashed (which it does with unnerving regularity).

I commented to my dear friend Susan, who is a single mother, "I don't know how you do this *all* the time!" She looked at me with gritty wisdom in her eyes and said, "You just do it—one day at a time, sometimes one hour at a time, sometimes one minute at a time." Indeed, her determination and commitment to do the best job she can in her work and as a single mom has given me strength to meet each of my temporary single-parenting days saying, "I can and will do this, and I will do it well!" My thanks to Susan for inspiring me to persevere.

I'm deeply grateful for the initial encouragement of Dr. Brian

Newman. After reviewing the early, very rough draft of *Keeping Your Family Close,* he gave insights, suggestions, and validation that set my hands to the keyboard to continue scoping out the topic with renewed enthusiasm.

I also want to express my gratitude to Rev. Stephen Macchia for challenging me to excellence in writing this book. His belief in this topic as a family issue, long before others saw his cutting-edge vision, encouraged me to knock harder on doors for good questions and dig deeper for honest answers.

It seems trite and too ordinary to say that this book would not have borne fruit without my editor and agent Leslie Stobbe. But the truth is, he believed in the validity of this issue, and the book would not have developed without his mentoring. Because of his gentle insistence, I restructured and rewrote much of the original manuscript. As I cut, pruned, and complied, and the manuscript rose to his standards, he gathered my thoughts and words and presented the topic to others with personal conviction. I thank him for his steadfastness and faithfulness to me and this book.

My special thanks goes to those of you who shared your experiences and feelings with me over coffee, in your homes, in restaurants, after workshops, and over the telephone. Without your stories and your personal insights, this book would have been flat, void of depth, and very one-sided. You helped me take this idea and expand it, making the information inclusive and accessible to many more people than I could have done alone. You each know who you are, and I thank you.

And lastly, Peter. What can I say? It's ironic that the travel that keeps us apart is the very thing that brought us together for the writing of this book. Thank you for working out all these issues with me. Thank you for listening, sometimes repeatedly to the same frustrations over and over. Thank you for talking, sometimes seemingly endlessly. Thank you for being my biggest fan, my personal cheerleader, and my best friend. I miss you when you are away.

Introduction

Road warriors. Just the name implies people in battle, carrying heavy burdens of armor, fortified for protection, aggressively forging onward. But what are they fighting for? Who are they fighting against?

The media coined the phrase "road warrior," and *The New York Times* (May 14, 1995) defined it as anyone who takes fifty or more flights a year and has an equal number of hotel stays. It makes one wonder if the people who qualify as road warriors are possibly fighting for their own identities! People meeting these criteria spend more time in planes, airports, rental cars, hotels, and meetings than they do in their own living rooms. Just what home and family really mean has become a little hazy.

Perhaps the battle road warriors wage isn't against the pressures of travel at all. For Christian men and women who travel, the battle is to live within their priorities, balancing family, church, ministry, and profession.

Are you or is your spouse a road warrior? Even if this definition doesn't fit the travel separations you experience, you likely have skirmishes in your life related to business travel. Otherwise you wouldn't be reading these words.

Hertz Gold #1, National Emerald Aisle, Admiral's Club, Hilton

Honors, Marriott Miles, frequent flier program—which ones do you or your spouse belong to? Oh, I know, they make a businessperson's life on the road more bearable, easier. The perks and initiatives enable the traveler to concentrate on business, not on how he or she will get there.

But the convenience and ease by which businesspeople are able to travel unhindered around the country and internationally has contributed to one of the greatest inconveniences to families. Why? Because sometimes traveling and being away is easier than being at home facing family responsibilities and issues. Ah, the question of true identity returns. Does one derive his identity from his family or his work? And to whom does the business traveler's time belong—his family or his employer?

On the opposite end of the identity tug-of-war is the spouse left at home. Married in name, he or she is actually singularly bearing the weight of home and child-rearing. Married for love and life, the person at home might not feel prepared for intermittent separations and the isolation of being a part-time, nontraditional single parent. Misunderstandings and confusion of expectations and roles provide fodder for battles between such couples.

At this moment, whether you are standing in a bookstore, sitting on an airplane, or reclining in a chair in your living room, you may be wondering if there are solutions to the issues you face because of business separations. You might be feeling some bumps along the route your marriage is taking, perhaps finding you have less to talk about with your spouse when you are together, feeling dwindling intimacy, and developing more and more interests your spouse doesn't share. Maybe you are wondering if other couples have struggled also with separations.

Peter and I pondered these same things. We looked for guidance in reading material and found very little. We shouldered our way through the problems and committed ourselves to reaching the other side of the jungle. We did indeed find our way to the proverbial greener pasture, but it wasn't without practically scratching and clawing our way at times. It was a grimy journey.

I set out to write articles about how we persevered, and having an analytical mind, I broke down our battles into manageable tactics that I could share with others. The problem was, the more I immersed myself in the project, and the more reading I did, and the more people I talked to, the more convinced I became that what I had to say could not be said in 2,500 words or less. What started as articles to document our own solutions exploded into more than 40,000 words to aid others in forging through the littered path behind us. You are holding the result in your hands.

I can say with conviction that Peter's business travel and the consequent time that he is absent from our family is the best and worst thing that has happened to our marriage and family. It has forced us to be "one" even when we are thousands of miles apart. There have been times when I wished for a "normal" family (or perhaps I should say "ideal"), one where Dad comes home at six, puts his feet up, reads the paper, has dinner with his family, prays with his children at their bedtime, and engages in some conversation with his wife before going to sleep.

But all is not "normal" or ideal in any household, and particularly not for families separated by travel. For husbands and wives who are apart because of business, a typical family evening consists of eating alone or with the children, coercing young children to bed, feeling inadequate to meet the emotional needs of teenagers, and finally crawling between two cold sheets, feeling exhausted and alone.

How can husbands, wives, and children possibly stay together spiritually and emotionally if they aren't together physically?

God designed relationships and marriage to meet our deep need for companionship. Remember, in the Garden of Eden after the Lord had created plants and animals, He was still lonely for fellowship, someone to share the joy and beauty of His workmanship. So He created Adam and then Eve, first as His companions and then, second, as partners for each other.

Because this original design was born of God's desire for companionship, it is an innate part of our God-given nature. We were not created to live in isolation. "In the Lord, however, woman is not independent of man, nor is man independent of woman" (1 Corinthians 11:11). We need each other; we complement each other. We all need the closeness of another person to talk to, touch, and see.

Business travel interrupts this communion between husbands and wives. Just when you have a connection with your spouse or feel you are on the verge of an intimacy breakthrough, off dashes one of you on a business trip. You've gained ground before the absence, but once you are back together, you may feel you've taken a few strides backward. Sounds a bit like the childhood game of Red Light/Green Light. How frustrating! This wasn't one of my favorite games as a child, and it's even less fun playing emotional Red Light/Green Light as an adult.

While you may feel that you are in a chronic on-hold pattern during business separations, I assure you that there are solutions. There are things you can do that will help release you both from this freeze frame. I think you'll find the insights and suggestions in this book doable and applicable.

Though I've written mostly from my perspective as a woman with a traveling husband, I've talked with enough families where Mom travels and Dad stokes the home fires to have an understanding of both sides of the issues. Regardless of which role you play, my prayer is that this book will equip you with the tools, confidence, and desire to stay close as a family when business travel keeps you apart.

1

Out of Town

THE MUSCLES IN MY ARMS AND UPPER BACK STRAINED AND burned from exertion. Tears of frustration and sweat mingled and tickled my cheeks as I pulled the frozen barn door with all my strength. I kicked it with my heavily insulated boots and pounded on it with my gloved hands. The two-hundred-pound door, that in the summer slid effortlessly on its overhead metal track, was hopelessly and relentlessly stuck in the below-zero cold. I tried one more time to simultaneously lift and pull the door. It didn't give an inch. I collapsed on the cold concrete floor and leaned against the unyielding door in complete exhaustion. "Peter, I need you! Why," I wailed, "did you have to leave me now? At this time of year! I can't do this!"

My plea was answered by the small voice of then six-year-old Geneva. "Mommy, can I help you? Mommy, please get up. We can do it!" I looked at my child, bundled from her nose to her toes, and thought of the trust and faith she must have in my ability and her strength to win this battle with the stubborn door.

I wiped the tears on my coat sleeve, and they froze immediately in place. I stood up and sighed. "Okay, honey, let's try it." We both grasped the door, and I placed my foot up on the door frame for more leverage. We heaved, and a prayer escaped my throat: "Lord!" The door moved an inch. We heaved again, and it moved six inches. Then I slid it back closed slightly and yanked back again quickly. Finally it gave up the fight and slid open enough for me to lead the horses out through the opening. I smiled thinly and whispered, "Thank You, Lord," knowing I would have the same battle eight hours later in the evening to close the door.

The frozen-door scenario was played out at least two dozen times over the course of Peter's two-week business trip to Russia. He was gone during January, which happens to be the darkest, coldest, and most brutal month of the year in New Hampshire. During his trip New England experienced (or rather survived) record cold of minus thirty degrees, true northeastern winds, and nearly daily snowfall. The elements caused a vicious battle within me in an already raging, bitter war.

The symbolism of the frozen door wasn't obvious to me right away. It was only later, in retrospect, that I saw what the Lord was trying to teach me. I was that frozen door. Before Peter left, while he was away, and even for a few days after he returned home, I was freezing him out. I didn't like to admit I needed him. Then I felt angry at him because I did need him! The Lord had to show me in this tangible way that I had some significant thawing to do before I could give Peter my blessing every time he headed off on a business trip.

The anger and frustration at Peter's travel schedule nearly overwhelmed me numerous times, but I made a conscious choice not to give in to them. Many, many emotions course through my vulnerable and fragile psyche, threatening to discourage me permanently. Sometimes an out-loud verbal reminder to myself is necessary to waylay negative emotions. I give myself pep talks, tell myself to buck up, and I talk to the Lord out loud. Hearing myself say the words into the air forces me to take accountability for what I'm feeling, disallowing any blame of anyone else. And then I try to do something about it.

Perhaps you, too, have experienced overwhelming moments when your spouse is away. Maybe you haven't. Every person involved in the family of a traveling person is bound to feel something. The emotion may even be guilt for not missing him or her! Regardless of what you feel, you are not alone.

When a woman's husband is away, she may feel as if she is trying to swim through a muddy bog. It's frustrating, unpleasant, grimy, and sometimes downright stinky. Between the isolation of parenting alone and the fatigue of shouldering all the household responsibilities, it's no wonder some women resent their spouses' time away from home!

Consider my friend Sara's situation.

Sara left home early, striking out on her own with enthusiasm and the anticipation of getting a college education. It took her six years to work and earn her degree in physical therapy. She married in her mid-twenties and worked full time to support her husband while he attended graduate school. Even after he earned his master's degree and they had two children, she continued to work part time in the evenings because she liked her job, thrived on the interaction with her patients, and it gave her esteem-building time away from home.

Their life ran smoothly until her husband accepted a job with an international sales group. After a cross-country move, she found herself without a job, mothering preschoolers and elementary-aged children, and living in a house that was frequently without the voice or presence of her husband. She realized that financially she didn't need to work, plus she felt she couldn't return to work and leave her children in day care. She knew that with her husband gone so much, it was important for the children to have their mother accessible as a constant in their lives.

Sara felt bound to her home somewhat against her will and recognized that her self-esteem was starting to plummet. She complained, "I feel like I live on a fault line. I can't plan anything for my life or pursue my interests because of his work schedule. Sometimes we don't have any notice of when he will be leaving for another trip, and the hassles of getting a sitter on short notice for any plans I may have had aren't worth the stress it causes me or the kids. I feel totally out of control of my life and what I can or can't plan!"

Don't you just hear the resentment and anger rising in her voice? She is precariously straddling an uneven line between her personal life and her marriage. The weight of one side rests in her need to feel useful practicing her skills in the workforce; the weight of the other side is pulling her toward her commitments to her family. She feels that her husband's travel schedule is like an earthquake, threatening her self-esteem and possibly sending her into a bottomless pit.

Shaky Marriages

I have felt those same tremors underfoot. Peter and I know the intense issues that inhibit the lives of a family when a dad is away frequently on business. The unpredictability of life without Peter makes me feel edgy. Plus it seems that something always goes wrong when he is gone. In my honest attempt to keep everything under control, I get overtired, which easily leads to loneliness and depression. Peter misses us when he is away, feels guilty for being gone, and feels out of the loop of our lives. We forget how to communicate well over the phone and sometimes find ourselves in deep silence, angry that we don't understand each other's feelings in our opposite situations. Bristling emotions circle our silences.

Travel-related separations become a lifestyle. Much the way habits are formed—good or bad—methods of dealing with separations will determine cycles within your marriage. These can be dealt with in a productive and healthy way, or they can lead to unresolved conflicts that will tear away at the very foundation of the marriage.

In 1994 the U.S. Travel Data Center reported that nearly forty million men and women travel on business every year. Considering that the population is still growing, and companies are also growing, that number is likely to swell. With an increase in the number of families experiencing a traveling spouse, we may see a surge in family breakdown and failure.

It's inevitable that the stress of an absent spouse will cause the demise of some marriages. Too many ambitious, career-oriented businesspeople inadvertently choose work over family. An unconscious neglect of spouse and children can only lead one way—to the graveyard of divorce. Though travel is necessary in some jobs, it doesn't mean a family has to suffer or disintegrate during these times.

You and I know that marriages are worth preserving. Peter and

I have talked with numerous friends and acquaintances about how they deal with frequent short separations from their spouses. Most people express bare minimum coping strategies. We know there is a better way. The approach in this book is traditional in nature, in that most families and couples we talked with are of the kind where Dad travels and Mom maintains the home front (whether she works outside of the home or not), though moms who travel are included, too. However, the principles of how a family relates and copes are unchanging regardless of who does the traveling.

Several more references are forthcoming about the trip Peter took to Russia in January of 1994. This particular separation was one of the most difficult times for us, but it resulted in a positive turning point in the way we handle travel. The Russia trip was the flicker of an idea and the impetus for this book.

While preparing to write about traveling spouses, I read and researched numerous books for added understanding of marriage and communication. I came across a letter Peter had written me in 1992. He wrote it while sitting at Kennedy Airport waiting to board a plane for home, and he had tucked the two pages into the flyleaf of a book he had been reading. In part he wrote, "I'm going to ask some honest questions about us, our relationship, our children, and our living situation. Please answer them honestly for me, hopefully before I leave for Chicago. Let's talk before then if possible."

Peter listed more than twenty questions, nearly half of which were related to his travel schedule. He never showed the letter to me, and I didn't find it for three years! But the interesting part is that his questions were intuitive, thought-provoking, and timely. I'm only sorry it has taken me years to answer them for him! A few of the questions were truly heart-wrenching as he searched for the correct balance of family, work, and church. Though the scale does sometimes tip precariously to one side or the other, we have learned through constant reevaluation to talk, listen, and compromise.

The following pages are Peter's and my insights into the tensions, issues, and emotions of individuals and families who experience the temporary separation of a parent or spouse due to travel. A trip doesn't necessarily involve an airplane or even business. It may just be an overnight or two at a Christian retreat, a conference, or a visit to a relative. But there are two sides to the "travel relationship," and each person must be willing to communicate his or her feelings about any trip to make it a success for all. (Traveling together or with the children is a whole different topic!)

We are committed to helping you to do more than cope during your spouse's absence. We'll discuss how your past has influenced your current coping mechanisms. We'll help both the traveler and the left-at-home spouse identify feelings about the times of separation. We'll talk about your marriage building and incorporating travel as a positive relationship factor. We'll ask you to think about how and what to communicate with each other. We'll encourage you to care for yourselves in healthy ways. We'll offer practical tips on how to honor, respect, and love one another despite physical distances. And we believe that if you accept business separations as a lifestyle the Lord has designed for the enrichment of your marriage, the threatening jagged edge of travel will be softened.

This is basically a book about one specific detail of marriage. Wonderful Christian books abound about the marriage relationship—by James Dobson, Bill Hybels, Chuck Swindoll, Gary Smalley, John Trent, Josh McDowell, and the Minirth-Meier people—to name a few. They offer invaluable insights into the entire marriage picture, while with this book I hope to add a few defining details to the canvas of married life.

For Discussion

1. In what ways do you feel your spouse's travel schedule affects you?
2. Do either or both of you feel you have developed patterns of coping with the times apart? Do you feel these patterns are healthy and productive or damaging?
3. Write down what each of you hopes to gain from reading this book.

Family-Building Resources

Below are "Ten Ways to Show Love from Afar" as thought joggers for the person who travels. (Hint: These can be used the other way around, too—generated from the person at home to the person traveling.) Think of your own ways also. One word of caution: You may need to check with the other person first about some of these suggestions. Don't be surprised if he or she doesn't like surprises!

1. Send flowers, chocolates, or balloons to your spouse's place of work.
2. Dedicate a song to your spouse on a favorite radio station.
3. Arrange for a dinner to be delivered, homemade from a friend or a restaurant.
4. Employ friends to "kidnap" her for a girls' night out (or him for a guys' night out). Arrange child care, too!
5. Sing a love song to your spouse on the answering machine.
6. Write a poem or a few sentences about why you love your spouse and send or fax them to him or her.

7. Before you leave, plant encouraging notes or verses around the house for your spouse to find.
8. Arrange for someone to come in to help clean the house.
9. Watch a favorite TV show "together" on the phone.
10. Tell your spouse you love him or her at least three times during a telephone conversation.

2

On the Road Again

THE FOLLOWING STORY IS NOTHING NEW OR UNKNOWN IN THE world of business travel. Does it sound familiar?

Harry is an interim minister. He and Kathy have been married for thirty-five years and have four grown children. For a number of years he was a senior pastor at one church, but as the retirement years approached, he wanted to minister to churches in transition. He opted to return to seminary to train as an interim minister. After completing the training, Harry and Kathy traveled around the country to stay briefly with different churches.

Five years later Kathy was ready to establish a permanent residence they could call home. They found and bought a perfect retirement house, but Harry had one more six-month commitment to fulfill in another state. He would get home only about once every six weeks. Harry and Kathy discussed it. Would it be okay for her to remain at their new house while he finished his last job? Kathy felt reluctant to leave their dream retirement home and move, even temporarily, so they figured, "no problem," he would live in the other state and fly home as often as he could.

You can probably write the rest of the story yourself. Because Harry spent more time in a faraway city than he spent at home, he developed deeper relationships with his coworkers and parishioners. One was a divorced, middle-aged, very emotionally needy woman. Though he had never even contemplated an affair, it "just happened." The long-term damage to his wife and grown children after just a few months of sleeping with this woman was nearly insurmountable.

Obviously, there had to be problems within his marriage to have this happen. But he also, at some point, made a conscious choice. He lost sight of his marriage commitment and retirement plans during his affair.

Sometimes it's easier to ignore problems, shut down communication, delve into individual interests (that exclude your spouse), and silently—and sometimes very quickly—drift apart. Plain and simple, a marriage takes supreme effort and time, and if we don't make a conscious choice to keep interaction going, a marriage will disintegrate.

This is why marriages that experience times of separation due to travel are extremely prone to ruin. Do you know one of the most often cited reasons for divorce in the entertainment world and in politics? Extended separations due to travel for work. In 1995 alone three marriages of freshman members of Congress broke up (*Wall Street Journal,* December 22, 1995) specifically because of the unpredictable nature of being civil servants, working for their country away from their families.

Ah, but we are Christians, you may be thinking. True, this may help protect you, and certainly your commitment to and belief in your marriage vows are strong. But you are no less vulnerable to

Satan's attack on families. He has already grasped the secular world by the throat. He concentrates even harder on Christians, setting into motion all sorts of difficult circumstances for you to conquer during separations.

These trying situations and circumstances can create such strong feelings of ineptitude and inability to cope that you may feel like shutting down emotionally. In chapter 1 I mentioned how learned and ingrained patterns of coping affect us. A complicating factor is your emotional, spiritual, and family history.

How you were raised, who parented you, what discipline style was enforced, how you coped with stress as a child, how your parents coped with difficulties, and even where you grew up and matured have all shaped you into who you are now and have affected how you cope with life's ups and downs.

Let me tell you a little more about Peter and myself as I reflect on our family histories and how these relate to who we are as individuals and our way of communicating with one another.

My elementary and preteen years were spent in a small Massachusetts town. My two older sisters and I relied on each other for company and friendship, since our closest neighbors lived about half a mile away. We developed a deep love of the four seasons, animals, and nature in the pine forests and fields that surrounded our home. The stillness about us fostered introspection and daydreaming. I loved the solitude and silence and felt closest to the Lord when deep in the woods surrounded by His creation.

When I was very young, my father traveled occasionally for his family-owned textile mill. Even as a child, I sensed he disliked his work and the travel, and I wasn't dismayed when he changed his life course and opened his own carpentry shop. Our family viewed his change as a "back-to-the-land" adventure. From that point on, my dad rarely took any trips alone. He worked out of the barn and was always accessible to the family. When we moved to New Hampshire the year I turned thirteen, he continued his carpentry business, which is still flourishing today.

By contrast, Peter grew up outside of Chicago in a strong Dutch Christian Reformed community. When he was young, the suburbs were safe, clean, and divided only by frequent golf courses. His father owned his own business of concrete repair, and from an early age Peter worked with and for his father "mud jacking." Peter learned a strong work ethic. He enjoyed the physical toil and especially liked meeting new people at different job sites all over the Chicago area. After high school, he went to Trinity College to pursue a degree in physical education.

Peter and I fell in love while on a college-sponsored European study trip about the Reformation. He was still a student at Trinity, and I was between colleges. We literally met for the first time on the airplane while en route to our initial destination of Brussels. It was a whirlwind tour (neither of us remember much of the text of the course) and a romantic adventure as we discovered that it wasn't happenstance for us to meet the way we did.

God's plan for us to be united in marriage became evident to both of us before the eight-week trip was over. While in Worms, Germany, Peter asked me what I wanted out of life. Looking into his deep, clear, green eyes and then glancing at his bright blond hair, I said, "I want green-eyed, blond children." He looked back at my similar features and said, "Me too."

Upon returning to the United States, I went back to New Hampshire to pursue a degree in nursing, and Peter continued his physical education degree in Chicago. He proposed to me formally a year later, and he moved to New Hampshire. We married in 1983, two years to the day after we met and three weeks after I graduated from nursing school.

We now live in a rural New England town with a population of about 1,400. We have two beautiful children (both with blond hair and green eyes)—Geneva Beth (whom we often call "Genna") and Jordan Peter. A menagerie of animals including three dogs, three cats, and four horses have made our home into a miniature farm—all of this much to my delight.

Peter and I both believe everything happens for a purpose—God's purpose. His perfect (and sometimes humorous) plan for us started on a trip. As it turned out, Peter's business trips were destined to be an integral part of our lives, something we couldn't have known at the outset.

Peter's traveling started benignly enough. He owned a concrete company (similar to his father's in Chicago) and worked throughout New England, occasionally traveling for an overnight or two. He switched jobs shortly after Geneva was born. The company he worked for required him to travel to teach other people how to operate a technical concrete machine. He would be gone up to a couple of weeks at a time.

At one point during these years he was working on a job in Chicago for several weeks and staying with his parents. I became frustrated coping with the farm, a one-year-old child, and my part-time job. One day an acquaintance at the local market commented that she hadn't seen Peter for several days. Without much thought I snapped, "He doesn't live here anymore." The woman looked surprised but didn't say anything. I couldn't let it drop though. "He has moved to Chicago, and he'll just be coming back for visits!" Taken aback at the venom behind my words, the woman wordlessly pushed my bag of groceries across the counter to me.

That evening I considered why I had reacted so angrily. I had made it sound like I had been abandoned. I thought of all the emotions I experienced every time Peter left on a trip, while he was gone, and when he came home. I started a mental memo of a pattern of my feelings and realized how much I resented his travel. Then I decided to attempt to decipher why I felt the way I did about his business trips. It was a slow process.

He accepted his next job offer the same week I found out I was pregnant with Jordan. The new job with a relief procurement agency would still require some traveling, but he was assured he would be able to create his own schedule. This held true for the most part, until he had to take a three-day trip when Jordan was six weeks old. I remember feeling scared, alone, and depressed. I wondered if other moms felt this way. I began to ask friends at church how they dealt with their husbands' traveling schedules. Most of the women expressed negative emotions and confusion about how to cope.

Now Peter is the president of his own Christian supply and logistics company. He says the guilt he experiences from being away is compounded because he now has complete control over his own schedule, but he must travel to keep the company afloat. The age-old conflict between priorities of family and work arises. Of course his family is tops after the Lord, but to support his family he must temporarily abandon us occasionally. What irony!

Willie Nelson's song "On the Road Again" begins: "On the road again; I just can't wait to get on the road again." I've always had a sneaking suspicion Peter hums this quietly to himself while preparing for a trip. I've had to face it—he enjoys his travels. Yes, he does miss us and feels guilty about leaving us, but he enjoys being "out in the world" too. Because of our differences in personality, his travel is actually a camouflaged blessing. He needs contact with people. Conversation and interaction pour energy and sustenance into him. He thrives in crowds, in being part of a bigger picture. He enjoys going to sporting events as much for the contact with people as for the actual game itself. Because of the isolation where we live and the tiny community we are a part of, he sometimes chomps at the bit for more interaction.

I, on the other hand, intensely dislike crowds. Even without speaking to anyone, I become exhausted in a crowded room. It's as if the energy in my body is drained just being in the presence of too many people. Even church can be a tiring place for me. I rarely go to large gatherings or sporting events because they are extremely stressful for me.

Peter and I are a true example of how opposites attract. One of the reasons I fell in love with him in Europe was his ability to talk to anyone anywhere despite language barriers. I felt in awe of his gregariousness. Though my awe has waned a bit (an unfortunate result of fourteen years of marriage), I admire, respect, and accept his need for people. And he offers me the same courtesy about my desire for solitude.

It might seem that I would actually like it when Peter is away. After all, I have never been afraid of being alone and rarely crave the presence of other people. But, of course, Peter is more than just another person. He has become a part of me and I a part of him. So when he is away, I feel that something is missing—his stability and presence in our home.

Over the course of the last ten years, we have developed positive ways to cope with being separated. By acknowledging and accepting our different personalities, we have recognized that it is actually good for us to be apart. We have the capability to injure one another emotionally because of our opposite personalities. Instead the Lord provided an alternative for us to learn to love and appreciate our differences. Our ability to cope and grow has matured through travel, and so can yours.

How You Cope

Coping skills are developed over the course of a lifetime and are modified with new input. An infant learns to cope with being hungry by crying, which brings his mother and food; a teenager copes with peer pressure by saying no to drugs and therefore grows in the ability to make responsible decisions through the college years; an adult loses a parent to cancer and learns to move through the grieving process and come out emotionally intact on the other side.

Life lessons like these start in grade school when the class bully pushes a child. How that child responds will determine how he will cope with a similar situation next time. If a child shrinks back and cries, he has learned only how to be bullied and scared. However, if a child stands up for himself, he learns to take responsibility for himself and gains self-esteem, not to mention respect from others.

The way you deal with any change or crisis is greatly influenced by how you have coped with similar situations in the past. The Chinese interpretation of the word *crisis* means "danger" plus "opportunity." During your spouse's absence, your mind may perceive the separation as a time of danger or vulnerability. But also you have an opportunity to discover how you will manage. Will you deal with it effectively and thereby positively equip yourself for future separations, or will you become figuratively immobile until he or she returns? Each trip may not involve an actual "crisis." However, from an emotional standpoint, every trip calls for a new level of coping.

This new level can be a positive step up in a maturing of your coping skills, or it can be a negative spiral into self-pity. If your tendency is to hibernate emotionally whenever your spouse leaves, you will not gain the coping skills you need to function independently. But if you are able to grow and mature during times of separation, your coping ability increases with each trip.

Your Personality

Your individual personality traits and tendencies can strengthen your marriage during a trip or tear it down. People may be categorized broadly as introverts or extroverts. Introverts tend to be thinkers. They watch the world (somewhat suspiciously) and let information pour into them from all five senses. They respond only after processing all the facts. Crowds, noise, and a lot of action exhaust introverts, and they frequently seek out times alone. Extroverts, on the other hand, gather information quickly, process it, and talk all at the same time. They love action and being in the thick of it. They gain energy from crowds and other people.

However, personalities are much more complicated than simply being introverted or extroverted. People can be strong-willed, self-assured, determined, stubborn, shy, timid, guilty, funny, serious, rigid, structured, rebellious, disciplined, willing, perfectionistic—the list could go on and on. God gave us our individual personalities, and He has yet to run out of combinations, making each person distinct and unique.

Each trait will contribute positively or negatively to your coping skills when a spouse travels. For example, a strong-willed person (who can be an introvert or an extrovert) will have the ability to withstand time apart from his or her spouse because of the determination to see things through. This type of person likes challenges and rises to the occasion in most situations. He or she has an inherent resolve and generally is persistent in the drive to survive and grow. If you live with or are a strong-willed person, the words "bullheaded" sound familiar! A strong-willed person may dislike the absence of the spouse but will rarely let those feelings interfere with the acts of parenting, working, or maintaining the home.

However, self-centeredness may actually drive the overly confident, strong-willed person. When selfishness undermines a marriage, the other person's feelings can be overlooked. The marriage cannot survive a self-centered traveler or a blindly determined stay-at-home spouse.

Certain personality traits could overpower a loving and giving marriage, and precautions need to be taken to prevent possible problems. Both an overdependence or extreme independence can hinder necessary adjustment and growth in a relationship.

Of course, men and women are innately different, too. Those sex differences alone will influence how you both look at a situation. I like the Proverbs 31 woman. Verse 16 says of her: "She considers a field and buys it . . . " Not that I would ever buy a field without Peter's consent, but I have spent time "considering" fields.

A couple of summers ago I attended a horse show by myself

in Vermont. I love these times I spend "vacationing" with my horse. Part of the daily routine includes rising in the hush of sunrise to drive to the barn to feed my horse and prepare him for his classes. One morning as I traveled down a rural dirt road, early morning mist clung to a large, grassy field; needles of sunlight sparkled on the dewy grass. I thought how much more beautiful the field would be if a few horses were peacefully grazing in the tranquil setting.

As I rounded a bend in the road and lost sight of the field, it occurred to me that if Peter "considered" the same field, he would immediately want to know what was under the grass and dirt. Was there gravel? Was it rich loam? Could the field produce a profit if it were "turned over"? My conjecture about our opposite responses to this lovely, idyllic field made me laugh. So it is in our marriage. I can predict that we will have nearly opposite views of circumstances almost invariably. Sound familiar? Makes life interesting, doesn't it?

So it may be with the way you and your spouse view your times apart. Recognizing that you will look at them differently, cope with them differently, and possibly have opposing issues to deal with starts the process in the right direction.

Your Family History

Another factor influencing the way you both deal with frequent times apart is your family history. If a parent was gone often when you were a child, you probably have unconscious and various ways of coping with a loved one's absence. These childhood memories may spark strong negative feelings. Perhaps the traveling parent was verbally or sexually abusive, and you felt relief when he was gone. Or maybe the frustrated parent left at home battered you whenever your other parent traveled, which contributed to feelings of vulnerability and abandonment.

The truth about family history is that it repeats itself, for better and for worse. Inner-city welfare recipients frequently beget welfare recipients; poverty is handed down as an inheritance, and physical and verbal abuse become a way of handling anger and frustration.

Consider the woman who as a child was constantly berated about her appearance or for her attempts to play sports. Until she finds her worth in Christ, she will likely struggle with a poor self-image. Her low self-esteem will spill over into the way she relates to her children, coming out in criticalness and even self-criticism. People raised in an atmosphere of constant criticism have a difficult time receiving and giving praise because they never learned how to say or hear positive words.

So it is with abuse. People raised in abusive homes need to gain healing from the past and learn skills to keep from passing on the abuse to their own children. They need to change the abusive coping mechanisms they were inadvertently taught.

If you have unpleasant memories from childhood, whether in relation to a parent traveling or not, those feelings and recollections can alter your perspective on your present situation, and they need to be addressed, through books on Christian living, your pastor, or a trained counselor.

On the other hand, family history can have a positive influence. Perhaps your dad traveled a lot when you were a child, but your fondest memories are of his return home and his attentiveness and interaction with you. Or maybe you planned elaborate homecoming parties for him. Pleasant memories offer a more positive view of the issue and are a good source to draw on.

As Peter and I have delved into our own family histories and the way they relate to our current relationship, how we cope and why we react the way we do have become clear. Seeing the present in the context of the past has given us a much deeper understanding of one another. And as we have employed spiritual, Christ-centered truths to build our overall marriage, we have learned and are continuing to perfect what we call our "travel relationship." It's an area of mutual respect and understanding of our differences. It is how we support and honor one another while we are together and separate. It is the growth and maintenance of a cohesive Christian marriage.

For Discussion

1. Write down your own family travel history. Discuss and compare each of your perceptions of the travel schedule in your family.
2. Talk about how your feelings have changed concerning business-related travel over the course of time.
3. Discuss how your individual personalities tie into your feelings about the travel schedule.
4. Discuss any family history that may influence how you cope with your spouse's current travel schedule.

Family-Building Resources

Bill Hybels wrote a terrific book titled *Fit to Be Tied* about personality differences and expectations people bring into marriage. Even if you have passed the decade (or decades) mark in your relationship, read this book. It will help you go beyond mere tolerance of each other's differences.

3

What Is the "Travel Relationship"?

SINCE HISTORY FREQUENTLY REPEATS ITSELF, ONE WOULD THINK that people would learn its lessons well. However, many times we don't, and that is why these lessons may take on greater significance with each passing decade or century. Take a moment with me to page back in time to see how travel has affected us historically.

The biblical history of travel begins with the banishment of Adam and Eve from the Garden of Eden. Until the first couple fell into sin and wandered down the path of no return, they had a permanent home in Eden. There was no need for them to leave the garden before Eve sank her teeth into the juicy fruit. God had designed them, their lives, and the garden to be perfectly suited for one another. Why leave when perfection and all provision was at their doorstep?

But leave they did. The Lord had no choice but to banish them and force them to become wanderers. Then along came the Flood, wiping out the Lord's entire creation, save Noah, his immediate family, the paired animals, and sea creatures. Noah drifted on the high seas for probably another ten months after the rain stopped. He had no idea where the Lord intended him to land and disembark, but he was obedient and willing to build the ark, secure the animals, and float aimlessly. His travel plan was completely out of his hands but ordained by God.

As the world began to repopulate, travel for commerce, marriages, funerals, wars, and celebrations was commonplace. The quickest means of transport to anywhere was by chariot or horseback. It took weeks and even months to reach the final destinations. What a frustrating life it may have been to realize that a letter wouldn't reach its recipient any sooner than if it was hand-delivered by the writer! This was the way of life for the kings, prophets, and common people. Travel was a necessity that few people thought of as an inconvenience and probably never considered a curse.

I don't say that traveling was then or is now a curse. Nor am I implying that current business-related travel is the same as spiritual wandering. However, if we allow a spouse's business travel to determine our emotions and relationships, it can become a curse. Deuteronomy 11:26-28 says, "See, I am setting before you today a blessing and a curse—the blessing if you obey the commands of the Lord your God that I am giving you today; the curse if you disobey the commands of the Lord your God and turn from the way that I command you today. . . . "

These words from Moses to the Israelites during their years of wanderings are no less relevant now, because we can choose to obey God's commands and receive a blessing, or we can dishonor the Lord by disobeying the commands and receive a curse. Allowing a divisive wedge to come into your marriage because of unresolved conflict due to travel schedules is dishonoring to the marriage vows you made before God on your wedding day. Don't permit a curse of this sort to undermine your marriage!

In the New Testament, the most amazing revelation about travel comes with Joseph and Mary's journey to Bethlehem. Jesus came into the world on a trip. Incredible, isn't it? The couple had traveled far from home knowing the baby would be born during the journey. The symbolism of Jesus' birth in a dirty and humble stable is obvious. However, the symbolism of the trip to get there is overlooked. Jesus' birth, so far from the comfort of a familiar setting, speaks of our continued lack of a permanent home. (It is only because of His death that we are guaranteed a final and everlasting home in heaven.) Also, the wise men traveled an incredible distance and length of time (some scholars say up to two years!) to see Jesus. Again, a metaphor of how we can only be saved by God's grace through a spiritual journey that ends at the feet of Christ.

As Jesus grew and began to minister, He and the disciples traveled extensively, never owning a long-term residence. After Jesus was crucified, the disciples continued the ministry of Christ, thereby becoming the first Christian traveling salesmen. They journeyed hundreds of miles on foot year round. They stayed in touch with loved ones through letters, and, despite not seeing many of their churches for extended periods of time, their love increased—an important point to remember when our own loved ones travel.

Frequently our relationship with the Lord is referred to as a "walk" or journey. We are always on the move with Him. He is forever leading us somewhere. Much of the time we may not know where He is taking us, but we develop faith to continue following Him—to pursue His itinerary for us. It is as if He has given us a map for our trip with Him, but He only gives us directions as we come to intersections where we must make choices. And through these choices, we become more like Him and less prone to sin. Our earthly travels continue until we die, because we will never reach the unattainable pinnacle of perfection here on earth. Like the Israelites, we find our spiritual travels to be ongoing and never ceasing.

The changes that have taken place since biblical times are beyond anything the disciples could have comprehended. We can communicate overseas directly by phone or fax; generally speaking, we can fly anywhere in the world in less than twenty-four hours, and letters within the continental United States rarely take more than a few days to reach a destination. We have become very high tech—and consequently impatient. We don't like waiting, wandering, or wasting time. We want clear, concise, and predictable forms of communication and travel. We have become intolerant and restless victims of our own so-called technological progress.

This impatience is nowhere more evident than in marriage relationships, where "me first" has usurped "us" and "we." We want the perfect marriage without the struggle of the sometimes painful journey. Our independent streaks are shaking the ground and foundation upon which our marriages are built.

The Marriage Building

There are many levels of the marriage relationship, and much has been written about each level in one form or another. Marriage has been compared to the seasons of nature, parallel train tracks, and artwork—to name a few. Because of our desire to make ideas tangible, Peter and I think and speak of our marriage as a building.

Ephesians 2:20-22 says, "Built on the foundation of the apostles and prophets, with Christ Jesus himself as the chief cornerstone. In him the whole building is joined together and rises to become a holy temple in the Lord. And in him you too are being built together to become a dwelling in which God lives by his Spirit."

In today's world the holy temple of marriage can be likened to a skyscraper. The foundation, set on deeply embedded concrete pilings that rest on granite, is rock solid when it includes the undergirding of Christ as its base. The tower of a positive marriage grows each year, adding new floors, layers, and patterns in the shape of children, jobs, ministry, work, etc. The uppermost levels will be buffeted by storms and winds, but with Christ as the cornerstone, the building won't crumble.

The primary or the weight-holding levels of a marriage can be divided into six sections. First and most obvious is the base of an individual, personal commitment to and relationship with Jesus Christ. The five levels beyond this can be viewed as: 1) your mutual spiritual relationship, 2) your sexual relationship, 3) your emotional relationship, 4) your parenting relationship, and 5) your financial relationship. Each has its own rewards, concerns, and problems—pretty standard for every Christian family.

I don't claim to be an expert in all these areas, and some very good comprehensive books have been written about them. However, we need to look at each level briefly to form a better understanding of how they work together to uphold the building of marriage. And we want to see how each relationship level subtly affects and is affected by a spouse who must occasionally leave the construction site of your marriage for business trips.

The Spiritual Relationship

The spiritual relationship goes beyond your individual personal commitment to Jesus Christ. It concerns how you relate to one another on a spiritual level—your mutual walk and growth in the

Lord. People grow in the faith at different rates, but a couple's joint growth or expansion is the continuum upon which their lives are nurtured and matured.

Dr. James C. Dobson wrote in his book about marriage, *Love for a Lifetime*: "Finally, the Christian way of life lends stability to marriage because its principles and values naturally produce harmony. When put into action, Christian teaching emphasizes giving to others, self-discipline, obedience to divine commandments, conformity to the laws of man, and love and fidelity between a husband and wife. It is a shield against addictions to alcohol, pornography, gambling, materialism, and other behaviors which could be damaging to the relationship. Is it any wonder that a Christ-centered relationship is the ground floor of a marriage?"

As usual, well put, Dr. Dobson! It is through prayer, devotions, and discussions that your spiritual bond strengthens. And a mutual growth in the Lord provides a stronger unit to face all the storms that will blow against your family.

Psalm 127:1 is a reminder of the need for the Lord to be the builder of your relationship: "Unless the Lord builds the house, its builders labor in vain. Unless the Lord watches over the city, the watchmen stand guard in vain." Every facet of your marriage relationship needs to be built from God's blueprint, because your humanness limits your ability to nurture a marriage alone.

The Sexual Relationship

God designed the sexual relationship for three reasons—for our supreme enjoyment, to unite us in flesh as one, and to continue the human race. The expression of intimacy through lovemaking is symbolic of the five other intertwined levels of your relationship.

The act of intercourse illustrates God's desire for us to be one flesh in all the other areas of our married lives. Sex brings you to the core of your very being as you are unabashedly vulnerable and transparent with one another. It is the ultimate unity builder.

The Emotional Relationship

Do you ever fight with your spouse and realize suddenly that your argument has taken a turn off of the rational road and has entered the narrow and muddy track of emotionalism? It happens to the best of us, generally as a form of self-defense. Somehow you feel violated, so you become critical of the other person. Unfortunately, it means you usually end up attacking the character of your spouse.

Having emotions and expressing emotions is not the problem. As we all know, it is how we express them that gets us in trouble. We each have a different way of showing how we feel. I wear my emotions on my sleeve. Everyone knows how I feel every minute. Peter tends to hide his feelings, and we have to really dig to float them to the surface.

How boring life would be if we all thought and acted the same way! Your emotions are part of what makes you you. Your individual emotional side consists of your instincts, reflexes, and gut reactions. Your emotions are heavily tied into your personality.

A number of years ago I decided to plant a summer garden. Peter built a raised bed for me and filled it with rich soil and fertilizer. I decided on just a few vegetables as a start, to see if I enjoyed it. I bought five leggy, young cherry tomato plants. I propped them up in the garden and planted peas, beans, parsley, and carrots around them. Everything grew fantastically, beyond what I had expected. But then the tomatoes began to take over. First they shaded and killed my parsley. Next they encroached on my peas, and finally they throttled my beans. I couldn't keep up with the fruit either. Soon beautiful red tomatoes were literally rotting on the vine. But what happened next taught me a life lesson. The rotting tomatoes began to affect everything else they came in contact with. A whole shoot with five or six tomatoes would succumb to rot just because of the presence of one rotten tomato. Profoundly like us! Just one of us has to have a rotten attitude, a wrong spirit, and everyone else around us is affected.

How you relate to one another emotionally will affect every other area of your lives together, too. When emotionalism takes over in every argument, it undermines your ability to deal rationally at any level with your spouse.

The Parenting Relationship

Before Peter and I were married, we adopted a puppy. We picked him out together, named him together, and attempted to train him together. I say attempted because our ideas of what trained meant were from two different worlds. The poor little puppy became frightened quickly of Peter's authoritarian ways of disciplining, and when the dog came whimpering to me, I treated him like a lost child. Consequently we ended up with a dog that ignores Peter's commands and climbs onto my lap—despite weighing eighty pounds. I'm glad it was on a dog we learned from our mistakes and not on a child.

What this taught us about our differing methods of discipline was invaluable. We learned to communicate about the ways we were raised and what elements we felt were important to teach our children. It taught us to be consistent and loving. As on the other levels, we have learned to be unified in our approach to parenting. Peter still tends to be a stronger disciplinarian on some things than I am, but we have struck a good balance that helps to maintain our children's equilibrium.

In his book *Honest to God,* Bill Hybels discusses the purpose of parenthood: "True followers of Jesus Christ don't have children merely for the fellowship factor. . . . They view parenting as the opportunity to invest themselves fully in the life of a child who will someday become an irresistible manifestation of God's grace and make a difference by exercising his or her unique talents and gifts."

As parents we have an awesome responsibility and calling in raising godly children, a role not to be taken lightly.

The Financial Relationship

Some people may consider the financial aspect of a marriage a necessary evil. Obviously we all must have money to operate in this society. The problems come in how we mesh our individual beliefs into our daily lives. How and what you spend money on tells a lot about who you are. A gregarious and outgoing person will generally be more free when dipping his hand in his pockets, whereas a shy or reserved person might be more thrifty.

Your financial relationship can make or break a marriage. Studies on divorce have reported that the two most common reasons cited for couples breaking up were sexual disagreements and financial problems. Not very surprising, really.

A continuous lack of funds destroys trust in the marriage. A woman may feel that she can't possibly be vulnerable and rely on her husband to take care of her if he can't keep money in his pocket or in the checkbook.

Josh McDowell's book *The Secret of Loving* says, "The very use or misuse of money can be a dynamic source of friction in every home. One careless or undisciplined partner can literally devastate a marriage by his or her poor control and use of money." He goes on to say, "A mature love, marriage, and sex relationship cannot function in a godly way in the day-to-day dealings of life without financial responsibility."

Working together on a strategy to maintain a balance in your financial concerns (and checkbook) is what the financial relationship consists of. The security of a working budget and financial plan offers long-term stability to the entire marriage.

Stability Shakers

All of these levels need to be intact for the others to function well. They are independent of each other but are also reliant on the stability of the others to be effective. If one is out of balance, all the other areas are affected.

All effective relationships are built on honesty and trust with good communication as the glue. Dishonesty in a marriage, whether it is lying about a small matter or having an extramarital affair, acts as a corrosive to the entire building. Though the erosion may not be evident to outsiders, dishonesty will eat away at the inside of the walls (or inside both spouses) until the structure is so fragile it takes only a breath of wind to collapse it.

Dishonesty can go undetected when there is a lack of communication or intentional miscommunication. Some people are naturally suspicious, but through adequate verbalization their concerns will be cleared. But continuous dishonesty will invariably lead to mistrust, which has the power to permanently destroy a marriage.

A couple we know, Tracy and Paul, were married young. From

the start they were plagued with financial problems. They had individual school loans and credit card debts to contend with. Both had good jobs, but they couldn't seem to keep up with the bills, never mind get ahead.

Paul began to take cash advances from his credit cards, without telling Tracy, to pay the bills. This went on for months until they were at their credit limits. Eventually Tracy caught on to what Paul was doing. She has confided to friends that she partly blamed herself for choosing to stay ignorant and closing her eyes to their financial problems. But she blamed Paul more.

Impending financial disaster nearly did permanent damage to their marriage. Tracy was mad at Paul and became emotional every time they tried to talk. He became defensive and downplayed the problems. Tracy felt that she couldn't trust Paul anymore, and she closed herself off physically from him. She felt he had let her down in the most primary way. He couldn't take care of her. Spiritually they collapsed and were unable to pray together. Every area of their lives was affected. The entire marriage building fell out of alignment because of dishonesty and mistrust.

Pyramids and Palaces

I'm sure you can remember times during the construction of your marriage skyscraper when you wondered if the "project," your unity, would ever be complete. We have found that because of Peter's travel, we have to constantly reevaluate and readjust where we are putting our energy.

I also take heart when I think about the time and effort required to raise the great buildings of history. Consider the pyramids of

Egypt. I am fascinated by them. The magnitude of the planning and work that went into the construction of each one is mind-boggling. Foresight and detailed plans were necessary. Problem-solving skills and ingenuity were indispensable to the creators and builders.

First Kings 6:38 and 7:1 tell us it took Solomon seven years to build the temple and thirteen years to build his palace. The repetitiveness and monotony of the work combined with the slow daily progress could have been depressing. Though there may have been times of discouragement or delays, he never gave up, and ultimately he reached his final goal. Furthermore, all of it was pleasing to God!

We are unaccustomed to long-term thought and planning. Patience and perseverance for decades resulted in the pyramids—structures that are nearly indestructible. The parallel between the pyramids, the temples, and the building of our own marriage relationship is obvious. It just takes time! And as the active verbs *being* and *become* from Ephesians 2:20-22 imply ("being built together to become a dwelling . . . "), marital unity is an ongoing process, possible only with the Lord as the construction manager.

The Travel Relationship

So how does traveling tie in to all of this? Because when a spouse travels on business on a regular basis, a sixth level needs to be instituted as a permanent fixture to the building. A spouse's travel needs to be cemented onto the steel beams of your married life, so it can be viewed as a functioning part of your daily lives. If the travel relationship remains on the outskirts of your relationship, hovering menacingly, it will never have the same ability to withstand storms as the other levels do. When the travel relationship isn't welcomed and embraced as a routine part of your lives, it can easily become a destructive affliction.

Most people consider a spouse's travel as an inconvenience. But if we look at it as a normal part of everyday living, it takes on a less threatening image. How many of us would consider one of the other levels of our marriage relationship as an inconvenience? We can't possibly because Jesus is our life and hope, sex is our enjoyment, our feelings are part of who we are, children are our delight, money is a necessity, and finally travel is our work. For the travel relationship to function correctly, all the other levels must be in proper working order too. The travel relationship is dependent on the stability of the entire marriage building.

So many people just endure travel separations; however, the travel relationship needs to be more than mere coping strategies. Consider what would happen if all you did to correct problems with your finances was to wring your hands and say, "Well, it will get better next week." Why is next week any better? The way to correct financial problems is to have a budget and a financial plan. A plan empowers you to take control, withdraw your hands from their useless position of holding each other, and put your fingers to work.

The same holds true in the travel relationship. You can't sit at home, immobilized by emotions, claiming it will be better when your spouse is home from a trip. The travel relationship must reflect the determination of both people to form a family that maintains the dynamics even when Dad or Mom is away. It is a blending of roles so that each member needs the other but has the authority and ability to function without the other. I know through the course of Peter's travel schedule that I have become more mature and independent. Not that I need Peter any less, but I am more capable and confident in my ability to manage at home when he is away.

For the occasional traveler, this may not be so important. If the spouse travels only a few times a year, the need to incorporate the travel relationship into your marriage building is not so crucial. Even so, it is necessary to look at all the issues that surround a spouse's travel and deal with them appropriately.

Peter and I are still working on achieving a steady traveling relationship. As with all the other levels in every marriage, we may have walls that occasionally crumble and require fresh concrete patches. But we challenge you to construct a new permanent level called the travel relationship to your marriage building. Layer it on for permanency. It will fit. We guarantee it.

For Discussion

1. Discuss what levels of your marriage building have been the most difficult for you to keep stabilized.
2. Discuss a time when you both felt your marriage building was out of balance, and what measures you took to rectify it.
3. Talk about ways you can welcome and embrace your travel relationship into your marriage.

Family-Building Resources

From the maps on the back pages of your Bible and the text of the Gospels, map out Jesus' journeys and then Paul's. Children and young adults might enjoy using a more comprehensive book such as *The New Bible Atlas*. This is a fun family project and gives a great respect for the amount of footsore traveling early Christians did!

The Secret of Loving by Josh McDowell outlines a point-by-point road to successful marriage. It's really no secret; the truths offered are time tested for long-lasting love.

4

Absence Makes the Heart Grow Fonder . . . Sort Of

THE AGE-OLD ADAGE, PROBABLY FROM WARTIME, "ABSENCE makes the heart grow fonder," can be accurate, depending on how long you have known your heartthrob. In the case of married couples who have had a few years together, birthed a few babies, and have car payments, jobs, etc., absences from one another might be a blessed break. It also might lead to a revised adage: "Absence makes the heart to wander." The first is positive; the second is negative, and neither really covers how a spouse feels who is left at home on a regular basis. I propose a third version: "Absence makes the heart to flounder."

When Peter was away, I sometimes felt like a fish out of water. I flopped about, desperately in need of his buoyancy in my life, while I vacillated between being angry that I had been left and missing him terribly. My emotions floundered because I said I was strong and capable of handling life without him temporarily; I didn't like to admit my need for his presence. The reality was, I was out of my element and my comfort zone trying to be a good and consistent parent to our children. I did not feel secure until he came home and nudged me back into my place of motherhood.

When any spouse travels, it is imperative for all the family members to take a look at the feelings exposed in anticipation of the trip as well as during the time the person is away. Recognizing and verbalizing the emotions helps to put them in proper perspective as well as to dilute any negativism.

Word Pictures

In the book *The Language of Love* by Gary Smalley and John Trent, the authors coined the phrase "emotional word pictures." A word picture is used to convey a deeper meaning in communication by "simultaneously engaging a person's thoughts and feelings." Communication of this sort incorporates a visual picture into what you are trying to say. The person you are speaking to sees an actual image in the mind's eye, complementing and accentuating the feelings behind the words. For example you could say, "I am mad." Since there are different levels of anger, that statement tells someone else very little about how you are feeling. However if you say, "I'm as mad as hornets in a stirred-up nest," the image of fiercely stinging, angry hornets comes to mind. You may even feel like running away from that kind of wrath.

As you consider the emotions husbands and wives feel when their spouses travel, try to think of a word picture that accurately describes them. My word picture from the beginning of this chapter (about feeling like a fish out of water) captured my feelings of being abandoned, left out, angry, and insecure.

Word pictures can be used for positive ideas, too. I frequently think of Peter as an oak tree because he is strong (physically, emotionally, and spiritually), tough, true to his word, and—you guessed it—stubborn. Consider a positive word picture for your spouse and share it with him or her.

His and Her Emotions When the Spouse Is Away

Women tend to feel emotions more intensely and for longer periods of time than men. A woman may also experience conflicting feelings, possibly resulting in confusion. I have sometimes felt angry and glad simultaneously when Peter is away. It seems like a contradiction, but I can be mad at him because I have to deal with a leaky faucet and glad at the same time for some quiet in the evening to take a bubble bath, and then angry again because of the drip, drip of the faucet while I soak!

Complicating a woman's natural vacillation of emotions is her rise and fall of hormone levels. I don't believe in using hormones as an excuse for unacceptable or inappropriate behavior; however, many women experience extreme swings in emotions premenstrually, while pregnant, and while lactating. During these times feelings can become overbearing to a point of emotional crisis. This is when it is necessary to have an outside means of support through friends, a doctor, or a counselor.

The most common emotions men and women experience when their spouses travel are listed below. Think about each one and honestly consider if and how these feelings may be triggered when your spouse is gone.

Anger

The anger of being left behind is natural. It may feel as if he has gone off to have fun while he stays in a hotel, has his meals cooked for him and his bed made for him—all while he doesn't even have to pick up his clothes. Talk about easy living! He gets to eat out every night and have plenty of adult conversation during the day. He can ball up his dirty laundry and throw it in the closet. He can leave wet towels all over the place, and someone will come along and pick them up without complaining. It may seem that he's being pampered. His work day sounds extremely appealing to a stay-at-home mother of young children and to working mothers as well.

The other element in the anger is a sense of having been intentionally and deliberately abandoned—like a temporary desertion. A women's rational side may say, "He has to travel as part of the business. It looks good on his resume," etc. But since women tend to react to stress on an emotional level, they can't help but feel uncared for and possibly rejected by his absence.

The circumstances surrounding a wife's travels are a major factor in how a man copes with her absence. If they are both career-oriented, he may not feel as many negative emotions. In fact, he may be her biggest supporter and fan of her career and travel. But if she has become the sole provider of the family out of necessity, his feelings of anger at himself and their circumstances may become a major source of discord between them.

Resentment

Jealousy and resentment are normal responses to what women perceive as the husband's going off to "have a good time." It used to annoy me when Peter would take his golf clubs on a trip with him. He was supposed to be working, not golfing! Again, on an emotional level, the hotel and its amenities can almost be perceived as a mistress. Most of his needs are taken care of, and he gets to bask in the luxury of it.

Women also tend to equate travel with romance. Look at the ads on TV or brochures from a travel agent. Clear blue water, endless beaches, bright sunny days, immaculate golf courses, and candlelit dinners are the images we see. Let all that brew in a woman's psyche, and we're in for some serious jealousy!

When the wife is the most significant or sole breadwinner in the family, a husband could easily resent the role she plays. A man is created and raised to desire to care for his family. His self-worth may be challenged by her job alone, and her travel may compound his sinking esteem. He could begin to blame her for his feelings, and resentment toward her and her job will rise uncontrollably.

Bitterness can easily follow on the heels of resentment, resulting in a deeply embedded emotion that is difficult to eradicate. Hebrews 12:15 says, "See to it that no one misses the grace of God and that no bitter root grows up to cause trouble and defile many." The dangers are clearly described here. Bitterness can infiltrate your marriage and home, possibly defiling your entire family. Don't cultivate and allow any anger and resentment to grow into a bitter root.

Our friends Ben and Martha have a unique way of fending off any resentment or jealousy of the other's traveling schedule. They call it the "equality of travel time." For every trip Ben takes, Martha takes one as well. Martha takes her beautiful sewing projects to fairs to sell and show at competitions. The shows can be up to a couple of hundred miles distant, requiring her to stay away from home for a few days. Though her trips tend to be for shorter periods of time, their agreement is this: If Ben travels five times a year, then Martha also will travel to craft fairs and shows on her own five times a year.

It works well for them and helps them keep a balance in parenting and home responsibilities.

Of course, this would not work for most couples, but some variation might. For every trip the spouse takes, the partner also receives some benefit or advantage—time off to do something with friends or relatives, time or money to pursue an interest, etc.

Fear

Peter and I have the same conversation before every one of his trips. It goes something like this:

Me: "How long is your flight?"

Peter: "A couple of hours to Chicago, a short layover, and then three hours to California."

I contemplate this for a few moments, calculating how long he will be in the air and the number of takeoffs and landings.

Me: "Is your life insurance paid?"

Peter: "Yes, dear." (with a smile)

It may seem a bit morbid, but it serves several purposes and helps to alleviate my anxiety. The conversation is really about my fear of losing him and of not being provided for. He obviously can't guarantee he will come back, but he can guarantee that the children and I will be cared for should he die.

Mortality is a fact. Fortunately, we both have the assurance of eternal life in heaven, but it is necessary to discuss these kinds of earthly details frequently. If you both don't already have wills, don't wait until your spouse gets back from the next trip. Do it now, before he or she leaves again.

Anxiety and worry are symptoms of fear. When we fill our lives with the "what ifs," we can become immobilized in a web of such worries. Satan delights in using our fear to make us doubt God's ability to take care of us. Over the years Isaiah 41:10 has provided me with comfort and assurance. "So do not fear, for I am with you; do not be dismayed, for I am your God. I will strengthen you and help you; I will uphold you with my righteous right hand." What a relief to see two "I-am" and two "I-will" statements from the Lord for my assurance!

Vulnerability

I hate feeling vulnerable. That is different from fear. It is a knowledge that other people could take advantage of me or our children while Peter is away. Consequently, I don't tell very many people when Peter is traveling.

We live about a mile down a dirt road with only three other families as neighbors. I am fairly self-confident in running the "farm" and maintaining our home. I am capable of all the chores (including stubborn frozen doors), but simply because I am a woman, I am vulnerable—vulnerable to stress, to my car breaking down, to illness, and, worst of all, to intruders. That is everyone's worst nightmare.

Once when Peter was in Chicago, two young men in a four-wheel-drive truck became stuck on a dirt track that forms our property line about fifty feet behind our house. I was unnerved. The dogs were barking at the noise of spinning tires in mud, and the children were crying, fearful I would leave them to go and help the two men. As I watched the truck from behind a curtain in the living room, the telephone rang. It was Peter. A divinely inspired intuition had precipitated his call. Even though he could do very little to help me physically, just the assurance of his voice was comforting. I gave him a play-by-play of the two men and their stuck truck for the next twenty minutes. They managed to winch themselves out and then continued down the bumpy, muddy trail. Not once had they even looked at the house or seen me at the window.

Think about and discuss ways in which your home is vulnerable. Then develop your own security system to meet your needs according to your schedule and where you live. It might be helpful for a nearby neighbor to be alerted to watch for any unusual activity whenever your spouse is traveling. Introduce yourselves to a few members of your police department and talk with them about ways to ensure your safety in the community where you live. A watch dog (huge responsibility!) can be used as an early warning alarm. Some families also invest in security systems that will report intruders directly to the police station.

Our friends who instituted equality of travel time, Martha and Ben, like to have two cars parked in the driveway when Ben travels. Despite the occasional inconvenience it may cause Martha to drive Ben to the airport, they feel two cars in the drive is a visual deterrent to any possible intruders, since it looks as if two people are home. Whatever method you decide on to ensure your safety, make sure the system works and that you feel comfortable with its effectiveness.

Our security system consists of three dogs. One, who is more likely to lick someone into submission than bite, and another, a very protective, eighty-pound mixed breed, offer a barking alarm (the third one doesn't bark) whenever they hear anything out of the ordinary. We also have become friends with a neighbor who happens to be a police officer. Even though he works in a neighboring town, Peter and I both know we could call him day or night, and he would be at our house within a matter of minutes—very comforting for all of us.

Loneliness

Having time alone can be good, but loneliness indicates that the solitude has been overcome by a sense of desertion. Some men and women really enjoy the evenings when their spouses are gone. It gives them an opportunity to catch up on reading, watching a sporting event on TV, or rest.

For many women separation from the spouse is more pronounced in the evening. Just his presence is missed. And if fear is a factor in being alone, nighttime can present the most challenging time of day. This loneliness and fear will also accentuate other feelings of anger, resentment, and vulnerability. What a weighty emotional pattern.

At such times it is helpful to have a group of supportive friends who can fill in the gaps. They can't replace your spouse's presence, but they can offer companionship over a cup of tea or a telephone conversation.

Guilt

Some women really *love it* when their spouse is away. The demands of cooking, cleaning, and laundry are lighter. My friend Marie says it is a welcome break when her husband travels—only about four times a year. Her family maintains a much looser schedule; they eat when and what they want; there is less squabbling, and it seems there is a more relaxed atmosphere in their home. Self-imposed and real expectations are minimized, and it can be a relief.

For families who experience a limited travel schedule, this is probably a pretty standard response. The traveling is still novel, and it is like an adventure when spouses are away. The challenge of "going it alone" is exciting. But if this perspective is expressed to a family that experiences frequent travel, the response may be surprised silence.

One should not expect the same response to frequent travel as to infrequent. Everyone reacts differently, and the families who experience frequent travel cannot understand the attitude of a family whose Mom or Dad travels less frequently. The wife of a husband who isn't away very often could begin to feel guilty and wonder what is wrong with her for being happy!

If you are secretly pleased when your spouse travels, you need to consider why. It may just be the novelty of temporarily living without him. That's great if you can have a healthy perspective and rise to the occasion. But others may realize that there are problems in the relationship, and the travel allows a reprieve. That in itself is okay, as long as both recognize and are working on the concerns of the marriage. However, if the travel has become a form of escape for both parties, counseling is definitely an option to consider.

When men travel extensively or for extended periods of time, some women say that life is actually easier when they are away. Routines with the children remain constant until husbands come home. Then they mess everything up! This, too, can cause feelings of guilt. Of course wives want their husbands home, but when they are home, life is chaotic. Try discussing the family's daily routine with him and even writing it down for him. This will help him to "fit in" more quickly when he is back in the family fold.

Another couple we know, Angela and Andrew, experienced prolonged times of separation while Andrew was in his medical residency. Their one child was a toddler, and even though Andrew worked less than thirty miles away, he might as well have been three thousand miles away. Because of the nature of medical residencies, he was completely inaccessible to Angela and their daughter. He worked for twenty-four to thirty-six hours straight, and when he did come home, he was so exhausted that all he wanted to do was sleep. At this point Angela would either have to leave the house with their daughter or keep the toddler quiet.

No wonder Angela said it was easier when Andrew was gone! Her schedule with their child was fixed and worked well until Andrew showed up. Then they had to cater to his needs, which usually didn't fit in with their schedules. Angela and Andrew talked things through to make the lifestyle of a medical resident work for them. The result was that he slept at the hospital at the end of his shifts and came home when he was able to meld into his family's established routine.

Inadequacy

Feelings of inadequacy are common among men who maintain the home and children when a wife is traveling. He feels he isn't meeting society's standards by providing for his family and progressing toward making his mark in the world. This can be compounded by his feelings of ineptitude in being a house-husband. He feels he doesn't measure up, and an inferiority complex may begin to undermine his masculinity. He also may feel he can't meet his children's emotional needs, particularly if they are very young.

Once inadequacy undermines self-esteem, it is difficult to regain feelings of competency in any area. Without a job providing personal worth, he may begin the descent into depression. (Of course, this situation reveals the need for him—and for all of us—to gain a sense of worth from his relationship with God and not from what he does, from his performance.)

Depression

A combination of any of the aforementioned emotions can lead to depression. Because in our society people constantly pursue happiness and self-gratification, it is easy to fall into the trap of feeling less than "normal." When we somehow don't measure up to our own preconceived ideas of society's standards, we can become entangled in a web of negativism—that is, negative thoughts, self-doubt, and a feeling of hopelessness. Unexpressed feelings of anger, resentment, loneliness, rejection, and abandonment due to a spouse's travel schedule can easily lead to despair. Depression is more than feeling blue or down in the dumps for a couple of days. In the book *The Healthy Christian Life*, the authors describe depression as ". . . a loss of energy and motivation, a generalized feeling of pessimism. There may be such symptoms as a change in sleep patterns. . . . There may also be changes in appetite, a loss of confidence, and a sense of being overly self-focused."

Some people are more prone to depression than others. If any of the above negative feelings have been ongoing in your life, an increase in emotional demands will frequently lead further down the depression road. As I mentioned in chapter 2, your past will directly influence how you can currently cope with your spouse's traveling. If divorce was a factor in your childhood, you may have unrecognized feelings of abandonment. Or, if you have a history of physical or sexual abuse, suppressed anger and guilt can become overwhelming, manifesting themselves as uncontrollable rage or depression.

The first step in regaining control of the negative emotions and crawling out of depression is to recognize the problem and then take action. Communicating with a professional counselor is the best and most productive way to deal with chronic depression. You cannot and should not try to muddle through alone. If your feelings are totally overwhelming and confusing to you, seek help.

With each trip new feelings may surface according to where your spouse is traveling and how long he or she will be away. Old emotions, that you previously thought you had a handle on, may also surface and will require reassessment. Through all the ups and downs of the "travel relationship," remember it is the marriage relationship that needs to stay steady. Keep discussing and talking about your feelings to each other even as your spouse is stepping out the door.

For Discussion

1. List the three most prevalent negative emotions you experience during a temporary separation.
2. List the three most prevalent positive emotions you experience during a temporary separation.
3. Think of and discuss a word picture to describe how you feel. (Example: I feel like a fish out of water when Peter is away.)
4. Discuss specific ways to help waylay the negative emotions associated with a trip.

Family-Building Resources

For a more in-depth look at word pictures and how to use them effectively in any relationship, read *The Language of Love* by Gary Smalley and John Trent.

If you feel you have emotional wounds that need understanding and healing, consider reading *The Healthy Christian Life* by Frank Minirth, Paul Meier, Richard Meier, and Don Hawkins.

5

The Traveling Man and the Traveling Woman

THE TRADITIONAL ROLES OF A FATHER TRAVELING ON BUSINESS and a mother staying at home have become almost obsolete. Though Christian communities tend to support women who choose to stay home, the reality is, many women must work outside of their homes, and still others choose to maintain a career. The day is quickly approaching, and may already be here, when women will be traveling for business as much as men. Undoubtedly, with this alteration of roles, men and women who travel will be facing an increase of conflicting emotions. How do people experience travel, and what are their feelings about it?

A Trip to Chicago

When Geneva was a baby, I flew with her to Chicago to meet up with Peter while he was on a business trip. As she was under the age of two, she sat contentedly on my lap looking at books and playing with toys for most of the flight. The woman seated next to me obviously was a businesswoman. She wore a tailored suit and silk shirt and had short, easy-to-manage brown hair. She had been flipping through a report of some sort for most of the trip, but as we began our descent into Chicago, she began to sneak glances at Geneva. Finally, she smiled openly, and Geneva shyly hid her head on my shoulder.

The woman laughed and asked, "How old is she?"

"She's fifteen months and very shy," I answered.

"I know the age," the woman replied. "My little boy just turned two."

We went on to discuss briefly baby antics and milestones, and before we knew it, our plane was rolling to a stop at the gate. We stopped chatting and began to gather our personal items. She stuffed her report into her monogrammed briefcase. I crammed books and toys into the diaper bag. The businesswoman took one last look at Geneva and gently touched my child's hand. For an instant her eyes clung to Geneva's face, and then she glanced at me.

"I miss my little boy," she said quietly. Then she hoisted her briefcase on her shoulder, stood up, and stepped into the crowded aisle.

I saw her again at the baggage claim, suit bag in hand, confidently marching to the car rental desks. I marveled at her ability to leave her child behind for the sake of business. But then my marvel turned to pity. She was filling a dual and somewhat contradictory role. Was she content with the choices she had made? For the most part probably yes, but the sight of my child had touched her emotions and possibly her conscience.

How does any parent cope with the separation from children and spouse during business-related trips? Emotions, positive and negative, will influence how men and women experience and deal with travel. Dual and even triple roles are balanced during times apart, and the important factor in keeping the equilibrium is acknowledging and communicating feelings, as well as competently switching roles.

When Daddy Is Away

Not surprisingly the two most prevalent emotions a Christian dad feels when he is away on a business trip are fear and guilt. Like his wife, he fears an accident that could claim his life. His role in life is to provide for his wife and children. The threat of not being able to follow through on that commitment can cause fear. Even with a good life insurance policy, he knows money cannot replace his presence.

Peter says his fear of not returning home from a trip encourages him to keep his relationship with the Lord firm. He calls this his "other life insurance." Worrying does not help. "Who of you by worrying can add a single hour to his life?" (Matthew 6:27). What will help is knowing and living the truth that God is in charge and will always take care of each of us. God's perfect plan for everyone includes earthly death at some point. We cannot stop or delay His timing, so there really is no point in worrying about it. Our earthly responsibility requires us to have a daily walk with the Lord, be prepared for death, and anticipate ways to ensure that our family is cared for should one of us die.

Guilt

Hand in hand with fear is guilt. As I mentioned earlier, Peter's guilt is sometimes compounded since he has the ability to create his own schedule. He has struggled with the knowledge that his family is first, but for a time he was choosing his job over us. His guilt intensified when he knew I was feeling insecure about his being away. And the guilt deepened when he was away and he heard a negative report from home about sick kids, a hectic day, or a worn-out wife!

When Peter was preparing for his trip to Russia, he knew I felt that he was abandoning me. But he had to make a conscious decision to follow through on his commitment to the ministry he was working with. His commitment to God was first. He didn't want to leave us, but he truly had to.

About two months before he left, I was feeling particularly the anticipated stress of dealing with the farm alone in the dead of winter. I prayed not only for peace and assurance about Peter's being away, but I also asked specifically for help during his absence. I knew I needed help, but I also needed a definite promise from the Lord that He would be watching over me.

Peter was scheduled to leave in the middle of January, and I received a call from an acquaintance around the end of November. This young woman, not a Christian, asked if we had any room in our barn to board her horse for the rest of the winter. I hedged. I had asked the Lord for help, not more work! Then she shyly said she had one problem. She couldn't afford my boarding rate, so would I consider letting her work it off every month? An answer to my prayer in the form of a young lady needing and wanting to work for me! We worked out an arrangement that suited both of our needs.

As always the Lord's timing was perfect, and with this very specific response from Him, I knew Peter's trip was absolutely in God's will. My peace and acceptance of his trip greatly reduced his feeling of guilt.

Anger

A couple we know, Russ and Margaret, relate an experience with anger that could have thoroughly discouraged them. Russ had temporarily moved to California from the East Coast for five months. His company had paid for Margaret and their three children to move with him, and after the five-month commitment was over, they were happy to be returning home. They came back to the East expecting to settle into their home, and then Russ would return to his usual job. They arrived home on a Sunday afternoon. One hour later the phone rang. It was one of Russ's clients—could he please return to the West Coast immediately for an unspecified period of time? There was nobody else to do the job. He had to go. The family hadn't even unpacked yet!

The anger they both felt stayed with them for days, but he really couldn't say no. Margaret says now she wishes they had never answered the phone! But at the same time this particular unexpected trip helped them begin to accept his travel and learn not to hold a grudge against the company. When he returned from this trip, they discussed at length his job, their family, and their priorities. They mutually agreed that his career was important enough to endure the inconveniences of travel separations. They, in effect, permitted their travel relationship to become a permanent part of their lives and thus warded off potential damage to their marriage.

The guilt about a trip can turn into anger when a dad has no say about when and where he travels. Saying no to business travel can jeopardize advancement in the company or the job itself. A man may feel completely out of control of his own life and future, resulting in feelings of insecurity. These may drive him to use controlling or manipulative techniques on his wife or children. Add past baggage from difficult family relationships, trauma, or emotional pain, and the anger will spiral at a dizzying pace.

Suppressed anger tends to move in one of two directions—depression or rage. Neither is healthful or helpful. As we discussed earlier, depression is a symptom of a deeper problem that may require assistance from a professional. If anger is a significant and frequent emotion in your life, seek help. The emotional level of your marriage-building is out of balance, and you need outside objective intervention to realign it.

Anticipation

There is certainly an element of anticipation before any trip. A man may be looking forward to meeting new clients, visiting a new city, or learning about new concepts at a conference. The prospect of any of these things, plus being on his own in a new place, is exciting.

If he is a planner, he will have positive expectations of himself and his time away. However, the wife left at home may interpret this excitement as a desire to be away from her. The positive anticipation of the trip needs to be communicated for what it is—an excitement about the unknown and doing his job, not about leaving her.

Self-Satisfaction

Hand in hand with anticipation is the satisfaction of a job well done. Maybe he has been chosen to go to a conference for more training, or he has been selected to represent the company to some clients. These are positive self-esteem builders. Companies know that good self-esteem plus increased responsibility produce a motivated and successful employee. In essence the company is telling him, "We have complete confidence in you to represent us well. Go to it!" He needs and deserves this pat on the back.

Since Peter is the president of his own company, the self-satisfaction of his travel is even stronger. If he comes home from a business trip with a new client or order, of course he is going to be glad he went! It will encourage him to go back out again. And naturally I'm glad when he has successful trips, since it has a direct effect on our bank account.

The anticipation and consequent rewards from a trip end in positive results. Any business traveler's compensation, beyond financial, is contentment, gratification, and a sense of worth.

Loneliness

For men who are not naturally outgoing or gregarious, being away from their family and friends can be extremely lonely. They may even feel especially alone in a crowd. Despite being around numerous people all day, his business contacts don't know him the way his family does, and he may miss the depth of conversation and intimacy he shares with his family. Outgoing men too will miss the easy and familiar interaction with their families.

The loneliness for most men is especially intense at night when they may be thinking of what they would be doing if they were home—putting the children to bed, reading the paper, talking with their wives, even doing the dishes. They miss the predictable habits of their family, making them feel left out and alone.

Some of the loneliness can be waylaid by frequent contact with his family; however, there is a significant danger of feeling lonely in a strange city. It is easy to seek out other avenues of sharing or closeness in bars or clubs, but the temporary intimacy it might offer cannot replace his family's affection. In chapter 9 we will look in greater depth at the temptations men and women face during travel separations.

Jealousy

Loneliness can quickly change to jealousy if a husband feels his wife doesn't miss him or feel lonely herself. It stands to reason that a man sitting in a hotel room who calls home to hear a party or laughter in the background could feel a little jealous. He's gone, and he feels left out of the fun! He may resent his wife or children for having a good time without him. *Hey, aren't they supposed to feel sad about my absence?* he may be thinking. He needs to remember that this may be how his wife copes with her own loneliness. She may have asked friends over for her own self-preservation because she missed him.

A dad may feel envy about missing a child's important developmental milestone or a special church event. He may feel left out when an exciting event happens without his presence. Videotaping or recording some events can help to dispel those feelings, as will hearing about the event after the fact from the child or wife. A conscious effort to keep jealousy from turning into anger or hurt feelings will help to prevent emotional separation from his wife.

When Mommy Is Away

Women experience similar feelings as men, but because their innate and genetic roles in life, i.e., nurturing mother and caregiver, are so opposite from the providing role, they will probably have a different intensity of emotions.

As much as some women may dislike hearing this, God created women to be men's helpmates, to bear and raise children, and to maintain a household, in that order. Necessity has forced many women into the workplace, and others have chosen that option. I don't want to discuss the breadwinner versus breadmaker dilemma; I just want to point out the way God designed women. Understanding this design may help clear the sometimes confusing and contradictory emotions women may have due to travel.

Guilt

Most women who travel feel some degree of guilt about leaving their families. They may feel guilty about having to leave children with sitters for extended periods of time or about leaving spouses in total charge. They may also feel remorse at liking their jobs and in essence putting work before family. Their guilt is compounded when the spouse is left at home with the somewhat uncomfortable role of being the primary caregiver. If the husband feels abandoned and angry, the wife who travels can't help feeling guilty.

Honest and justifiable guilt is normal. It is the way our conscience tells us that an area in our lives isn't quite right. However, the guilt a woman experiences because of travel is trickier. It is an honest emotion, but is it necessary and healthful? Guilt is healthful when it comes from within, when the reason behind the feeling can be pinpointed, and when it can be dealt with objectively. In other words, a mom might say to herself, "I've worked hard on my degree to be able to have this type of job. Yes, I feel sad about leaving my children, but I feel this is what God has called me to do with the gifts and talents He has given me."

Guilt is not healthful when it is produced in a person by someone else. This scenario isn't fair for either person because neither is taking responsibility for his or her own emotions. If a husband blames his wife and her travel for his own feelings of anger or abandonment, he has diminished his own ability to cope, and he has laid unnecessary condemnation on her. His blaming may be subtle—through shutting down emotionally or physically, or direct—through verbal blame-laying, but it is self-centered and immature for him to react this way.

Nor is guilt helpful when it begins to influence other areas of life, thereby preventing objectivity. Guilt has the ability to immobilize one physically, emotionally, and spiritually. If you have begun to feel this level of guilt, counseling may be necessary to work out an objective solution.

Fear

Fear of traveling and leaving one's family is natural and may be expected. As I mentioned previously, fear of not returning is a father's greatest concern, and it's a mother's as well. This fear is a valid and realistic emotion. Second to God, our children and spouses are what we live for—to be with them, nurture them, and grow old with them. The threat of not being able to follow through on that desire is terrifying.

We want guarantees in life. We want assurance that if we step on a plane in Boston, we will reach our destination in Tampa unscathed. However, there are few absolutes and guarantees in this risky life. We are born, and we are destined to die. What we do with the time in between largely depends on our ability to accept our finite nature and ask and permit God to have control. The reality is, we are not in control of any area of our lives without Him!

Our friends Carol and John are separated by Carol's travel, as a nutritional consultant, for about 100 days a year. Their eight-year-old daughter has never known any other way of life. Mom travels on business. Period. Although travel is a regular part of their lives, Carol deals with a lot of fear of being out of control. They have excellent child-care arrangements; their daughter is well-adjusted; John is not only supportive but encouraging of Carol's career. So why does she feel out of control? Because she is not in charge of the daily happenings in life when she is away. She has had to learn to let God be the solid foundation of the marriage building, and He is the one ultimately responsible for the life of her daughter—a sobering and difficult concept to embrace.

Loneliness

Some women feel grateful and relieved when they have time alone on a business trip. The time spent by themselves in a hotel room may be so fulfilling and rejuvenating that it overpowers other negative emotions. Certainly to a stay-at-home mother, the prospect of uninterrupted time locked up in a hotel room is so appealing she may fantasize about "losing" the key!

But the novelty wears off for women who travel extensively. Living out of a suitcase and never feeling at home in a hotel may lead to loneliness. Because she misses her family, the loneliness is compounded by the guilt she may feel.

A man's loneliness may lead him to look for company in restaurants, bars, and theaters, and women may seek out these places as well. Unless a woman enjoys being alone (and many do), she, too, may go to people-filled places. If she is outgoing, she truly needs the hum of activity to lift her spirits and energize her.

Of course, a woman alone in an unfamiliar city is vulnerable. All it takes is one little slip, revealing that she is traveling alone on business, and she has opened the door for a potentially harmful situation. It is disconcerting that women must be suspicious and act defensively, but this must be the case for a woman to adequately protect herself.

Carol tells of a time when she was traveling with a group of people giving a seminar. She vaguely knew the other people but considered them acquaintances, not friends. One of the men started to show an interest in her and began to follow her everywhere when they were in public. Then he began to wait outside her hotel room in the morning to go to breakfast with her. She felt unnerved. After all, how well did she know this man? Eventually she asked one of the other women in the group to escort her everywhere. She realized that the label of "professional" meant very little in this case.

Women must find the balance between fulfilling a need for interaction with other people while traveling and avoiding dangerous situations. Personal safety measures will help to lessen the likelihood of assaults or robbery while still allowing contact with business associates and the city.

Self-satisfaction

A woman will take a great measure of pride in her work, particularly if she has labored for many years to obtain a degree or a place in the business world. Traveling for business can be considered a perk and a step up the corporate ladder. As with a man on business, a woman asked to represent her company will feel positive self-esteem because of her company's confidence in her.

Women who travel on business frequently tend to be very

focused and determined in their approach. Outside distractions will not deter them from the business tasks at hand. The mommy, wife, and Sunday school teacher hats are back at home in the closet. They are capable of locking up those roles until they return home. That doesn't mean they don't care about their families while they are gone. It simply means that they have complete confidence in the person left in charge at home. They may actually become better and more self-fulfilled persons because of the travel.

This self-satisfaction is positive for the whole family. Yes, children need their mothers, but some women are extremely goal-oriented and have high energy. Some are greatly gifted for ministries that reach far beyond their own families—for example, Amy Grant, Joni Tada, or Kay Arthur. These women truly need to work in order to fulfill God's calling on their lives. Traveling on business or for ministry is gratifying and even necessary for such women.

Both men and women will experience some negative and some positive emotions when they travel, though it is not surprising that the emotions may change with each trip. The extent and degree of the feelings will vary somewhat according to the length of time away, destination, and how the family at home is coping. Recognizing the factors that contribute to difficult emotions and talking about them will help to keep them to a minimum.

For Discussion

1. Discuss with your spouse the three most common negative emotions you feel when you are away.
2. Discuss how travel affects your self-esteem and self-satisfaction.
3. Talk about how you alleviate some of those feelings.

4. Think and talk about which emotions are most obvious during what times of day (i.e., loneliness is most noticeable in the evening).

Family-Building Resources

Traveling alone may make a person vulnerable. Women, especially, need to be cautious in an unfamiliar city. Here are some suggestions for personal protection.

Educate yourself about the city where you will be staying—enough so you know the main routes to and from the airport as well as the general layout of the neighborhood around your hotel. Never tell a cab driver it is your first time in a city. Some cabbies may take advantage of your lack of knowledge and rack up extra miles.

Never give out your hotel room number to anyone, including business associates. If you need to meet at the hotel, arrange to do so in the lobby or a restaurant.

Double-lock the hotel room door every time you enter and never prop the door open—even for a moment. Don't open the door to anyone, regardless of who they say they are, without checking their ID through the peephole or calling the front desk first for verification.

As soon as you check in, familiarize yourself with the closest exit (other than elevator). Always plan two different routes of escape should an emergency exit be required.

Don't leave any valuables in the room, including jewelry, money, passports, credit cards, etc. It is probably safer for women to leave all their valuable jewelry at home, other than their wedding band. Make use of the safe in the hotel room or at the front desk for any valuables or extra money you do not want to carry with you.

Try to stay in a hotel with an obvious security system. Ask

ahead of time what the security system consists of when making reservations over the phone. Women in particular should take advantage of security personnel and ask to be walked to their cars. Even better are hotels with valet parking. When valet parking or security guards aren't available, park in well-lit areas as close to an entrance as possible. Also consider carrying a personal protection device such as a whistle or pepper spray.

A more in-depth look at staying safe when traveling is *The Safe Tourist* by Leslie Windsor.

6

Can We Talk?

WHEN I WAS PREGNANT WITH GENEVA, I WAS EMPLOYED AS AN obstetrical nurse at the hospital where Peter and I would be delivering our baby. Despite my own knowledge of the birthing process, we attended childbirth classes. After the classes and as "The Day" approached, Peter felt confident in his ability to help me through labor. Just as our class instructor had suggested, we talked at length about our expectations from one another during labor and delivery. Secretly, I was concerned that Peter would be shocked by the intensity of the experience, but I knew he would manage to help me as best as he could.

My labor finally started late one night, and we arrived at the hospital around 2:00 A.M. I wasn't very far along in my labor but chose to remain at the hospital mostly because I felt safe surrounded by my coworkers and the familiar maternity ward. Around 6:00 A.M. I was exhausted and lapsed into brief naps between the contractions. Peter was tired, too. He thought I was sound asleep because my eyes were closed, so he crept out of the room—I assumed for a bathroom break. He didn't return for over an hour. In between the intensifying contractions, I became mad, concerned, and then frightened. He finally reappeared, a bag of doughnuts in hand. Then I became really angry. He had left me in labor with our first child for doughnuts! I'll admit that a surge in hormones played a part in my reaction; however, I felt abandoned during the most painful and terrifying experience of my life.

Several days later I was finally able to confront him rationally about it, and Peter was truly remorseful. He didn't think it would be an issue to me for him to run out to get something to eat. He had been up all night—he was hungry. He said we had never talked about my need for him to stay glued to my side during labor. Sheepishly I had to agree. Naturally I had assumed he would know not to leave me—and we all know what happens when you assume something of somebody. Almost invariably the opposite is true! Our miscommunication and downright lack of communication caused this scenario. Of course I have forgiven him, but ten years later I still can't forget.

How You Communicate

The buzzword from the 1980s was *communication.* From articles, books, and seminars everyone learned how to communicate with bosses, family, and best friends. We were taught how to discuss problems with our mates. Parents figured out how to talk to their children. We learned to decipher body language. We became bold in expressing ourselves. We talked, conversed, listened, clarified, reiterated, interacted, and dialogued through arguments, decisions, and dreams. We learned to listen with the two ears God gave us and speak with our mouth.

Communication isn't any less important now, and many

insightful and genuinely helpful books are still making the rounds to assist us in remaining good communicators. There is little I can add to all this. But in the context of learning to communicate effectively and thoroughly with a spouse who travels frequently, let's look at what type of communicators you and your spouse are and how you interact with one another.

Are You a Cup of Tea or a Pot of Coffee?

How you process information, written or spoken, is the first step in identifying your communication style. How you listen, hear, internalize, interpret, and respond to words is your way of communicating. I like to think of information-processing as either being a cup of tea or a pot of coffee.

A person who hears and processes words quickly is like a cup of tea. There you sit, a tea bag in a cup, waiting for the information (positive or negative) to pour over you. As soon as the water hits—instant brew! It doesn't take you long to hear or feel the words. The ideas, concepts, and impressions are quickly available in your mind. The process is nearly instantaneous. If you are a cup of tea, you will be ready with an answer, thought, or argument immediately.

A pot of coffee, on the other hand, takes time. Information pours in at the top of the percolator, your brain, which sifts through the ideas and thoughts. It takes several minutes for you to hear and understand the picture in its entirety. Once all the words have filtered through, it takes you a few more minutes to understand the concept and then even more time for you to form a coherent response.

The communication style needn't be an issue. Yes, the two

processes are very different and possibly frustrating when discussions take place between a coffeepot and a cup of tea. However, understanding which you are and which your spouse is will help you to be patient with each other. We need to allow our spouses to be who they are and to accept their communication styles.

Are You a Volcano or a Lake?

How do you respond to the information your mind has processed? A cup of tea communicator tends to be a volcanic responder. Your speech may be explosive, while your mind is running full steam ahead with words, images, thoughts, and ideas. Your mind may respond so fast that sometimes you have a hard time getting the words out of your mouth quickly enough. And your whole body becomes involved in the process through gesturing hands and intense facial expressions.

A pot of coffee generally is a lake responder and tends to be more peaceful. The ripple effect from the information continues throughout a conversation. Your speech and thoughts are slower, more controlled, and somewhat orderly. In your mind you have stacked up the ideas you want to discuss, and you present them in a systematic fashion.

There are certainly times when a pot of coffee personality will react in a volcanic way, as well as times when a cup of tea person will process thoughts and relate them more slowly. There is also a third way of responding—silence. Being tight-lipped and not talking is almost more destructive than exploding. When you internalize all your feelings and thoughts, they can erode your physical and mental health.

I know that learning to talk about feelings is not easy. A good way to start is to write down your emotions and then allow your spouse to read them. Learn to identify the style of communication you are comfortable with, and then work together to talk more effectively about your feelings.

The key to sorting through all the emotions surrounding the travel schedule is talk, talk, and talk some more. Guys, if your wife snaps at you two days before a trip because you forgot to take the garbage out, take a look at the whole picture. Maybe she is subconsciously expressing anticipated feelings of not being cared for. Ladies, if your husband blows the weekly budget to buy gifts for the kids three days before a trip, take into consideration the guilt he feels about leaving the family. When you put these actions into the context of an impending departure, the emotions behind the actions will be understandable.

Regardless of the way you talk with one another, you both need to learn to recognize exactly what you are trying to express even before speaking. To say simply, "I'm mad at you," is ineffective. You must tell what it is that has made you angry (without attacking the character of your spouse). Use the "I feel . . . when you . . . because" format to determine exactly what the emotions are. For example I might say to Peter, "*I feel* abandoned *when you* travel *because* I get tired when I'm left alone with our children." I've told him how I feel about a certain occurrence or situation and why I feel that way, all without attacking or blaming him. It is then our responsibility to work out a mutually satisfying solution.

You can use this same format for positive emotions, too. I can say to Peter, "*I feel* loved *when you* bring me flowers *because* it shows me you care about me."

When you can begin to talk about and process information and feelings about your spouse's traveling schedule, you'll find the times of separation becoming less ominous and more positive. Negative emotions may still arise, but they will become more tolerable and less threatening when they are identified, faced, and dealt with.

Solutions to Negative Emotions

The first step in gaining control of any emotion is simply to call it by name. I have found it helpful to keep a journal of what I'm feeling during specific times of day. Next time a business trip interrupts your family, each of you can try to write down every emotion you have during the day. For the person at home a pattern will emerge over a few days. From this process you will be able to develop a plan to reduce the negative emotions simply by anticipating them.

When I started keeping a journal, I found the pattern of my emotions changed according to where Peter was traveling (in the United States or abroad), my menstrual cycle, and even the time of year. I've learned that the worst time for Peter to be away, particularly overseas, is January and February. Peter has taken this into consideration when he plans his trips.

The daily pattern of my feelings was easier to pinpoint. Typically when Peter is away, the hours between 5 P.M. and 8 P.M. are my most difficult. The farm chores need to be done; the children must be fed and put to bed; and right about 6 P.M., when he would normally be arriving home, I am struck by an intense loneliness.

To prevent myself from catapulting headfirst into the pit of self-pity, I always plan my evening the morning before. Maybe there is a TV show I'm looking forward to watching, or a mesmerizing book awaits me during a soak in the tub. A specific plan can help to divert the overpowering emotions.

It also uplifts both of you if you can encourage your spouse in his trip. Remember how his self-esteem is boosted from traveling because his company/boss believes in him? Try the same philosophy in your approach. Tell him you are proud of him. Assure him of your confidence in his ability to complete the goals of the trip. It doesn't mean you'll miss him any less; it just assures him of your support of his job.

Support Groups

A mom left at home might consider starting a support group. Talk with other women in your community or church who have traveling husbands. Perhaps they, too, struggle during his trips and need friends to talk to about their concerns. It could be an informal group that meets irregularly, or it could take the form of a Bible study.

What has worked well for many women is contacting a few select friends, who understand the pressure of having a traveling spouse, and agree to touch base by phone a few times during his absence. A good friend of mine, Beth, had four young children, and her husband drove a truck five days a week. Now her husband works out of their home, but I know I can call her anytime when Peter is away for a sympathetic and totally understanding ear. She remembers what it was like. Validation of this sort is necessary for the tired and frustrated mom. (More on accountability and support groups in chapter 9.)

Another positive side to formulating friendships with other nontraveling moms is the possibility of switching children—you take care of hers along with yours for a while, and then send all of them to her. This is especially helpful if both husbands are out of town at the same time. You each get a well-deserved break of a few hours, in the long run enabling you to handle better the rest of his absence.

Counseling

Sometimes the emotions and feelings of husbands and wives are overwhelming and/or confusing. Both of you feel on edge before he leaves on a trip and after he returns. You can't seem to put your finger on exactly what is bothering you, but you know something is.

Most marriages at some point need an objective outsider to help both partners verbalize what they are feeling or experiencing. The sign of a healthy marriage is really two people who realize there is a problem and seek out help. An unhealthy marriage denies the problems until it is virtually too late to find a cure.

Proverbs 20:5 says, "The purposes of a man's heart are deep waters, but a man of understanding draws them out." We all sometimes need a man (or woman) of understanding to help us define and clarify feelings. Counseling doesn't need to be protracted or confined to a psychologist's office. Counsel or advice can come in a small group Bible study, an accountability group, or a few sessions with your pastor. The point is to encourage and enable both partners to express their feelings without fear of being criticized or being told that what they are feeling isn't "right." Every emotion is valid if it is truly what is felt. An emotion becomes invalid when the blame for the feeling is laid on another person.

If I blamed Peter for my feelings of insecurity because he travels, I would be wrong. My insecurities stemmed from my feelings of vulnerability when he was physically absent from our house.

Instead of blaming him, I have talked with him and found things to do that make me feel less vulnerable. Our discussions lead to two positive outcomes. He understands what I'm feeling and bases his actions on those feelings, and we've worked toward making our home a place where I can feel safe.

If you feel that you and your spouse are not adequately communicating, keep trying. Just a desire to talk is a giant step in the right direction. Discussing how you relate and process information opens the door to deeper and more fruitful talk. Thinking about and identifying the emotions you each experience when your spouse is gone on a trip will renew the communication between you.

For Discussion

1. Discuss communication styles with your spouse and determine each other's style. Are you a cup of tea or a pot of coffee?
2. Do you respond like a volcano or a lake?
3. Try using the "I feel . . . when you . . . because" format to communicate to your spouse two negative emotions and then two positive emotions.
4. Try to identify any patterns in your emotions during times of separation.
5. Talk with one another about the possible need for marital counseling and about how that option makes you both feel.

Family-Building Resources

Invest in a devotional book for couples. Peter and I have found two books not only helpful to our marriage but indispensable in keeping us mutually on our spiritual track: *Couples' Devotional Bible* and *Moments Together for Couples* by Dennis and Barbara Rainey.

Here is a hands-on project for both of you. Each of you hold a rubber band. Play with it as you talk. Stretch it, knot it, unknot it, ball it up, twist it around your fingers. Discuss in what ways the rubber band is like a marriage relationship. I'll give you an example: Our rubber band reminds me that often I need to s-t-r-e-t-c-h beyond myself to understand and encompass Peter's feelings. What ideas do you have?

7

He's Going, Going . . . Gone

WHEN PETER WAS PREPARING FOR A TRIP, I USED TO FEEL AS IF HE were up on an auction block, talking fast, looking for the best bid, scanning the crowd, and completely disinterested in me—the treasure sitting at his feet. His mind began a countdown before he left, anticipating what he needed to do, where he needed to go, and how he could make the best business deals. He felt impatient to be on his way, to move on to the next item of business. Meanwhile, in the shadows I felt forgotten and unheeded.

Because of these preparations, the anticipation of his trips caused the same emotions—abandonment, anger, fear—as when he was away. Only I felt the emotions more intensely because they were compacted into a fairly short period of time.

The Single-Parent Mode

For a number of years, about forty-eight hours before Peter left on a trip, I would begin my own broodingly silent countdown. He called it my "Single-Mommy Mode." His luggage came out of the closet, and I started to separate myself from him, physically, emotionally, and spiritually. I became pensive and short with him. I took charge of the children and shouldered my way between him and them. I grudgingly laundered the clothes he had set out that he needed to pack. I became a single mom with an uninvited guest in my house.

In essence my actions were saying, "Fine, you are going to desert me in the next day or two, so I'll beat you to it and reject you first!" When I was feeling rejected, I didn't like to admit I needed him. So I subconsciously cut him off, and my self-concerned actions told him I didn't need him. But I really did need him. Very much.

Peter recognized my responses for what they were, and he tried not to take it personally. Unfortunately, my actions sometimes led him to reject me as well. His attitude became: "She's rejecting me because she thinks I'm abandoning her, so I might as well really ignore her and just be on my way!" But the potential for bruising each other's spirit was significant, and I have learned to express my sadness about him leaving in more productive and honest ways.

I learned to simply say, "I'm going to miss you." Why is it so hard for some people to say this to each other? Because it opens the door wide for moments of vulnerability. If you are about to be rejected by his departure, why open yourself to more hurt? But it is a double whammy to both of you if the impending feelings of missing each other are overlooked or neglected. Both of you end up feeling deserted instead of feeling loved, needed, and wanted.

Packing

Have the two of you ever discussed who packs and why? For the wife the act of packing for her husband for his trip can trigger hostility, too. A friend of mine whose husband traveled all week long and was only home on weekends told me that she hated packing for him. She resented packing his things for a trip she wished he wasn't taking. Here she was packing for a romantic adventure that he would take without her. Some animosity is understandable!

On the other hand some women really enjoy packing for their husbands. They want to care for their spouses' needs and show them love (not to mention to be sure they have enough clean underwear and matching shirts and socks). Either way it really doesn't matter who does the packing as long as it is agreed upon after discussing it.

Some wives slip love notes or cards into their husbands' luggage for them to find when they unpack. This prospect could be very difficult for a women to do if she is angry about his travel. But the boost it gives him—that she was able to put her emotions aside enough to have forethought in planting a note for him—is immeasurable.

One item absolutely *must* accompany the traveler on every trip. All other articles of clothing, books, or toiletries can be replaced but this—a current photo of the family. A photograph of his wife, the children, or the whole family serves several purposes. It's not that the traveler will forget how they look, but a photo that carries a certain expression or a favorite memory will encourage positive reminiscing. A framed 5 x 7 placed on top of the TV or on the bedside table in the hotel room ensures that the traveler will fall asleep and wake up to their faces. Looking at the pictures while talking on the phone with the family helps to keep the phone calls more personal and less businesslike.

I rummaged through many photographs in search of just the

right ones to give Peter as a Christmas gift one year. I wanted him to have a pictorial remembrance of us that would ignite positive memories and even laughter every time he looked at them. The formal family pictures just weren't true to who we are, so I chose three photos, two of which were from a trip to Disney World. I'm in a swimsuit with Jordan perched on my hip. We are both suntanned and smiling. The picture of Geneva shows her joyously riding a bicycle. The third picture is of our dogs, relaxing on the front lawn, tongues hanging lazily out of their mouths. Each picture, though not exceptional in quality, shows our expressions clearly and brings to mind the stories behind them. The pictures are the last thing in the suitcase when he packs and the first thing out at his destination.

The Departure

Sometimes Peter has very early flights, which means he has to leave before the rest of us have awakened. This kind of departure is almost easier on us. I give him a bleary-eyed, slack-lipped kiss good-bye, and when I wake up, it seems a less sudden transition into temporary single parenting.

Other times he does leave during the day. This is when I try to be upbeat and pleasant about his departure. I rarely cry, not because I'm not sad, but because a clinging insecure good-bye frightens the children and compounds his guilt. He needs to know he will be missed, but he also needs to know I can function without him.

Consider how it makes him feel if there is a big emotional good-bye every time he leaves on a trip. The traveling is a part of his job, which is a means of provision for his family. He is feeling:

"I'm going out to hunt and gather for you, so why are you crying?" A bit prehistoric possibly, but with your tears you may undermine his drive to provide for his family.

Small children find the departure less painful if something exciting is planned to do right after he leaves or upon returning home from school. An ice cream cone or a trip to the playground helps to delay the "I miss Daddys." Plan something for yourself too. Enjoy an outing with a friend or have a special lunch during your break at work. Have something planned that will brighten the day of his departure.

The day Peter left for his Russian trip will be etched in our memories for years to come—partly because we knew in advance it would be an extremely difficult separation, but also because I failed to follow my own guidelines.

He was packed (he packs for himself) and lingering near the door, watching for his ride to the airport. I knew he was just anxious to be on his way, to start the mission adventure he had been working on and planning for nearly a year. The children and I had no special plans for the snowy, cold afternoon. His ride arrived, and we hugged good-bye. He kissed the children, and a heavy lump tightened my throat. He slipped out the door and closed it quietly behind him. I sank down in the living room chair. Six-year-old Geneva crawled into my lap, and Jordan played on the floor at my feet. Tears started to fall from Geneva's closed eyes.

Suddenly I saw Peter's gloves on the other chair across the small room. Knowing he would need them in the depth of a Russian winter, I jumped up to race across the room. If I was fast enough, I might catch him before the car pulled out of the driveway. In my hurry and with Geneva still in my arms, I failed to negotiate

Jordan on the floor. I tripped over him, sprawling headfirst into the chair with the gloves on them. I didn't drop Geneva in the whole sequence, so my hands were not free to shield my fall. My cheek took the full force of the hard-cornered chair. I couldn't help myself. I started to cry. Really cry. Geneva ran to the door and screamed out for her daddy to come back. He raced back in to find me sobbing on the floor, with his gloves clutched in my hands. He knelt down and hugged me again, making sure I was okay.

Then he said, "I *have* to go."

I nodded, trying to stem my tears. I held out the gloves. He shook his head and smiled a little. "I already took a different pair." He hugged us each again and left.

The three of us crying and curled up on the floor was his last sight of us. The bruise on my cheek lasted the entire two weeks. It was a tangible (and throbbing) reminder to myself and the children of the pain we felt in our separation from him. And I resolved to try to never again send him away with such a dismal, heart-wrenching good-bye scene.

Thinking negatively ahead of time about a trip and shutting one another out emotionally will make for a more difficult time of separation. Recognizing the emotions concerning the trip, talking about them, and implementing practical and positive ways to keep everything upbeat will help the whole family to stand securely on both feet when you say good-bye.

For Discussion

1. Discuss whether you separate yourselves from one another emotionally in anticipation of a trip.
2. Discuss who does the packing and why.

3. Discuss and implement ways to make every departure upbeat and more positive, especially for the children.

Family-Building Resources

Take your family on a picnic at your favorite park or national forest. Make it a fun day—bring the dog, roast marshmallows, play Frisbee, and just goof around. Pack the camera and a couple of rolls of film to take lots of action and candid pictures. From these pictures pick several to put into frames or a small photo album for Dad or Mom to take on business trips.

8

Home Alone

"WHEN IS DADDY COMING HOME?" SIX-YEAR-OLD GENEVA ASKED ME.

"Not soon enough!" I snapped, immediately regretting my sharp words when I saw her crestfallen face.

"Mommy, why do you get mad when Daddy is away?" she persisted.

A good question from a very perceptive little girl.

I hugged her and said, "Because I'm tired, and I miss Daddy's help with you and Jordan."

One of the greatest difficulties you may face when your spouse travels is the task of being a single parent. The transition from traditional parenting to singleness is strenuous at best and can be overwhelming. Your backup and support system may be limited to a tenuous, fragile phone wire. My friend Martha calls parenting during her husband's absences "nonstop parenting." Even if a mother works outside of her home, Martha is right. Hands-on parenting becomes exclusive, unremitting for the person remaining at home.

Rarely is single parenting a choice. Barbara Dafoe Whitehead, author of *The Divorce Culture,* says that nearly half of all children under eighteen years of age in the United States will be the innocent bystanders of their parents' divorce. Even in our own churches, it is common to have friends who are single parenting. And what I'm about to say may make them angry. Despite the risk of offending a few, I maintain that intermittent single parenting is harder than permanent single parenting, *because it is never full time either way*. Single parents develop long-term coping skills and support systems to aid them in their difficult situation. Not so with travel-separated parents. It can be a very lonely position. You may learn to "get by" as needed, but you don't have the same depth of coping as full-time single parents. That is why this book was written—to help people do more than cope during their spouses' absences.

The good news lies in the permanence of your "travel relationship." When this aspect of your marriage becomes a constant, you have the capability to maintain a two-parent family even when one is physically absent, because your parenting ability will no longer depend on the presence of the other person.

Discipline

Ephesians 6:1-2 and 4 says, "Children, obey your parents in the Lord, for this is right. Honor your father and mother. . . . Fathers, do not exasperate your children." These verses straightforwardly state that the responsibility of raising children is a dual job for husband and wife. One parent cannot discipline a child as effectively.

The greatest challenge within the context of temporary single parenting is discipline. If Dad is the major disciplinarian in the family, some struggles could arise when he is away. The time to deal with any discipline problems is before he leaves. Trying to backtrack and regain authority with an unruly child during your spouse's absence could be disastrous.

To maintain the dual role, be sure that both of you are united in your disciplinary actions. Any of the good parenting books say that both parents must be involved equally in discipline. The child needs to learn at an early age that going to Mom after Dad has said no will still meet with a negative response. If ten-year-old Johnny knows that when Dad is away, Mom will let him stay up late, he'll push every button and be up until midnight, resulting in a stressed (not to mention fatigued) mom and son. All children need structure and consistency, whether they are six months or sixteen years old.

If your teen has an unusual request to go to a party, on a date, or sleepover, try to take the time to discuss it over the phone with your spouse before giving an answer. Your judgment could be hazy, and you need the input before making a decision. Consulting with your spouse also gives him or her the opportunity to remain involved in the children's lives and simultaneously lets the child know that the absent parent still has an influence, even at two thousand miles away.

Most of Ben's business trips last about three to four days. However, two times a year Ben must leave Martha and the twins for up to ten days at a time to attend conferences and trade shows. Martha says the family is generally accustomed to the short trips; it is the longer ones she finds most difficult. Days six, seven, and eight are when her reserves are at the lowest, and intuitively the children know that this is the time to push every one of her buttons. She struggles with maintaining her composure and predetermined discipline measures.

Out-of-control feelings prevail when a spouse is gone for an extended period of time. The more emotionally and physically fatigued and drained you are, the more your judgment and resolve are affected. That is why it is necessary to be certain of your own mental, physical, and spiritual well-being (see chapter 10). Your personal resources and reserves need to be intact to handle the marathon of temporary single parenting.

The Children's Emotions

When thinking about temporary singleness and nonstop parenting, consider your children's emotions, too. They are probably experiencing some of the same emotions you feel when your spouse is away, but at an immature level.

When Ben and Martha's daughters were toddlers, they would crawl into Ben's suitcase as he was packing. It was the way these little girls could communicate that they would miss their dad. And how heart-wrenching for their parents to see and understand!

If children are old enough to identify and express verbally what they are feeling, sit down and talk with them as often as necessary. Their responses may even surprise you. Geneva will sometimes say she is glad when Daddy is away because I sleep on the couch (our living room is next to her bedroom), and I am therefore more accessible to her. My closer physical presence gives her added security.

Have younger children draw pictures or just talk about what they love about Daddy to help them express their emotions. When Jordan was three, he would frequently play "airplane" with his Legos. Sometimes the airplanes would even crash in his make-believe world. At first this upset me. Did he know something I didn't? Was he mad at Daddy for leaving? I realized this was just the way he worked out his anxiety, and not only was it normal for him to play like that, it was healthy too.

The time children will most likely miss their dad is in the evening. Families with young children especially miss the evening rituals of Daddy singing, praying, or reading a story before bedtime. Some creative dads prepare a tape of themselves reading a favorite Bible story or singing. If the children are old enough to read, maybe Dad could write short affirming notes for each child to read every day.

Help your children to view their father's absence in terms they can understand. Regardless of their age, have a map or atlas handy to show them where he has gone. By the age of six or seven most children will be able to conceptualize distances well enough to realize how far away New England is from, say, California. Maps offer a great opportunity for teaching states, capitals, commerce, and other countries, too.

Calendars help even the youngest child to understand the passage of time. Also it is a comfort to small children to know that the same sun and moon we see can see Daddy, too. The assurance that God knows where Daddy is and what he is doing every minute helps children to cope. Ask your child to pray for his trip. Even if their prayers are self-centered—praying for him to bring them a toy—praying for their parent teaches children about the Lord's faithfulness.

Older children may want to keep a journal or draw pictures of each day's happenings for Dad or Mom to read or see upon returning. Also, keep any schoolwork your child brings home and save it in a folder for the absent spouse. Set aside younger children's school drawings, middle grade children's math tests, or older children's writing papers—whatever they have to offer—for the other parent to look at with the children. A father's or mother's desire to know what has happened in the child's life during the absence has an immeasurable effect on the child's self-esteem.

I try to use Peter's trips as a teaching tool for Geneva and Jordan. When Peter is away, we have special place mats we use with the United States on one side and the world on the other. At mealtime we look at the maps and play a game to see who can find a state or country first. We also have several state games and puzzles. The games are generally ignored except when Dad is away. As soon as he leaves, the games, place mats, and puzzles sneak out of the closets and don't seem to find their way back until Peter comes home.

Make Life Simple

Kids thrive in a familiar routine. Attempt to keep the routines the same when Dad is away. Keeping the same bedtimes and mealtimes, especially for small children, helps to minimize stress.

If there are areas that can be simplified, do it!

Try having sandwiches and fruit for supper instead of a hot meal. Wear casual clothes to church rather than getting dressed up.

When Peter is working in town, he generally doesn't arrive home until about 6 P.M., which means we don't eat until 6:45 P.M. However, when he is away, the children and I will eat much earlier, which allows me time to feed them, clean up, and still accommodate their bedtime rituals, maybe even have some extra moments for cuddling to deal with any insecurities they are feeling.

Part of keeping life simple is learning to let the unimportant things go. So the house needs to be vacuumed, but it is 5:30 P.M. You're exhausted from working all day, and the kids are cranky. Who (other than yourself) is going to blame you if the floor stays hairy from the dog? Let it go! Try to keep self-expectations to a minimum and reduce stress. Nobody is asking you to keep the same fast pace in his absence (or during his home times either). Remember, you are single-handedly parenting and maintaining your home—a job usually accomplished by two.

When I'm single parenting, I feel as if I have been "doing" for everybody else but me. Anticipating and meeting the needs of the children, maintaining a schedule for the various animals that have individual requirements, and sustaining friendships drains me not just of physical energy but of emotional energy too. I have learned that I have to set limits, particularly in the evening, to keep from expending more energy through phone calls. Though well-meaning friends and family may call to "check in," often I just don't have the resources to draw on to hold a conversation. Even if it is a person to whom I know I can safely grumble, sometimes I need to be quiet and not explain anything to anybody. Quiet best helps me to rebuild my emotional reserves. To me, simplifying in the evening sometimes means not answering the phone.

Keep a Sense of Humor

Along with simplifying and letting the unimportant things slide is developing and keeping a humorous outlook. Stress and anxiety can steal the joy from everyday happenings. Try to see the lighter side of life by spending time with upbeat friends or even reading books by humorists. Laughter really is the best medicine. Studies have shown that endorphins (the body's natural "feel-good" chemicals) are released when we laugh.

I have learned that it is much better for my coping ability if I laugh in unexpected situations rather than cry. I remember one week when Peter was traveling overseas. He had left us each with sore throats, on the verge of heavy colds. Sure enough, Geneva didn't feel well enough to go to school one day. Her head was stuffy, and she was lethargic. Because illness always seems to travel in packs, predictably one of the dogs needed to go to the veterinarian that day, too. I bundled everyone into the car and went for our appointment. As the vet intently examined the dog, I looked across the room at my two children. Geneva's face was ashen, and she was trembling.

"What's wrong?" I asked her, startled by her appearance.

"Mommy, I feel dizzy and sick," she whispered.

I saw her start to fall back against the wall, and I raced across the room just in time to catch her slumping body. I half-dragged, half-carried her to the waiting room and laid her down with her feet up. As the color returned to her face and she stopped shaking, I started to laugh. I mean really laugh, a nearly hysterical laugh, one where the harder you try to stop, the worse it gets. Not that I thought it was funny Geneva had fainted. It was just the only way I could handle the situation. The alternative would have been to crawl up next to her on the bench and cry. Not surprisingly, after my giggles subsided, and the puzzled staff stopped staring, I felt much better and more capable of handling the rest of the day with a sick child and dog. Thank goodness for laughter as a release from a tense moment!

Martha, Ben, and the preschool-aged twins relate a funny story, too, that helped Martha learn to keep her sense of humor when Ben is away. They hadn't followed their own guidelines when Ben drove himself to the airport and left Martha with their other car, a pickup truck. A friend of Martha's asked to borrow the pickup briefly, and they traded, leaving Martha with a two-door convertible. Early that evening Martha noticed one of Ben's employees, Mark, leaving the office building adjacent to their house.

About half an hour later Martha received a panicked call from Mark. "Martha, I'm in jail. Could you come bail me out?"

"Mark, what happened?"

"It's a long story. Could you just come and bail me out?"

"What about your wife?" Martha asked.

A pause. "She hung up on me. Please, Martha, you are my only hope."

"Mark, my kids are in their pajamas, and I have no way of getting there. All I have is the convertible, and two car seats won't fit in it."

They talked more and decided on a plan. Martha called a friend to borrow a different car, went to a cash machine for the bail money, and trundled into the police department with two preschoolers in tow. She had every right to be angry, stressed, and impatient with Mark. Instead she made it an adventure for her children and was able to laugh at the circumstances.

Staying in Touch

About a week before Peter left for Russia, we were discussing how we could stay in touch. Phone calls would be difficult due to the time difference as well as the likelihood that he wouldn't be able to get a clear line. Also the expense would be daunting. He thought he had come up with the perfect solution when he said, "I'll just fax you."

I just about lost it! "You're going to fax me?" I yelled. "You're abandoning me for two weeks, and the only way I'm going to hear from you is through a fax?" I was incredulous. In effect I felt he had put me in the same category as his business associates—people he had to stay in touch with somehow but didn't really need to talk to. He felt chagrined after my tirade. He promised to try to call at least every third day, which would require him to wait until 11:00 P.M. Russian time. As it turned out, he did reach me by phone, just about every time he tried; plus he sent two faxes. The handwritten faxes were actually much more heartwarming than I expected. Seeing his little heart smiley face at the bottom of each one lifted my spirits.

Telephone Guidelines

One of the best ideas we have come up with to stay in contact is to predetermine the days and times Peter will call us. We write the times down on both of our daily planners and observe the "appointment" with the same seriousness as a visit to the doctor. This ensures that we won't play telephone tag and rules out any feelings of neglect. If I know in advance his call should be coming in around 5:30 P.M., then I won't be interrupted (hopefully) in the middle of something.

When Peter is in a different time zone, it seems as if he is especially far away. I feel as if he is on another planet. This is when it is really important to stay in touch. Too many times in all of our lives, out of sight means out of mind. He can't possibly know what is going on in the family's life, nor can I know how his business is going if we don't communicate daily. It could get expensive, but Peter and I both feel we can't put a dollar figure on our relationship. Also, we can't have a good relationship if we don't talk. We both need to know how each other's days have gone, plus what to pray for in the upcoming schedules. It helps to tell someone about the day's high and low points (without "dumping" too much). It is also imperative for the children to say at least a few words to Dad. It helps to keep him grounded in the reality of his family, and it lets the children know they are still important to him.

It is a good idea to establish some ground rules for telephone conversations while your spouse is away. In all families there are some potentially explosive subjects that should not be discussed over the phone during a business trip. If talk about finances always leads to arguments or disagreements when he is home, it certainly won't be better over the phone. The problem with phone calls is that you can't see the other person's body language or facial expressions. You can only hear the words and inflection of the voice. Unfortunately tone of voice and words alone are open to misinterpretation. Rarely do people talk with deadpan expressions, and we subconsciously rely on what we see to decipher what is being said. (Try closing your eyes while talking about a serious subject with your mate. I will venture to say that most of the time you can't keep them closed.)

Decide which subjects could be triggers for disagreements, and resolve not to talk about them over the phone. It may be finances, sex, discipline of the children, overeating, or any other likely controversial topic. Peter and I rarely discuss my work over the phone because it is a very intimate subject for me to talk about. I need to be able to see into his eyes and know he is looking into mine to be sure he is hearing what I am saying and so I can see his response.

Talk in advance about what sort of questions you need your spouse to ask you during phone conversations. Be sensitive to one another's need to talk about what is important to each person. Listen without interruption and ask good questions. Then switch to the other person. If one of you tends to monopolize phone conversations, set the timer for five or ten minutes for each of you to talk. A traveling dad may need to discuss his business meetings as a sort of debriefing. Some stay-at-home mothers of young children may not want to discuss whether little Johnny went pee on the potty today. She may need to discuss politics for ten minutes to give her a welcome break from motherhood. Don't expect your spouse to know what you need to talk about—tell him or her what questions to ask and what subjects to discuss!

Beepers and Other Means of Staying in Touch

Peter carries a beeper on his hip when he travels. The initial purpose of the little box was to provide a way his business associate in the office could reach him when there was a pressing concern. But Peter's beeper also allows us access to him all the time. We are no longer reliant on the prearranged phone calls (though we still call each other). We can contact him very quickly through the beeper. It has given me peace of mind to know I can track him down regardless of where he is (in the continental United States) and what time of day it is.

Some beeper companies allow rentals for brief periods of time. It may be worth the time and expense for your family to consider having the traveling spouse carry one along.

When you have access to computers, you can use the Internet and E-mail as forms of communication too. If privacy isn't a factor, this may be a good way to stay in touch. Also, research the possibility of a private 800 number for your home phone. Some families have found that an 800 number offers them significant savings on calls when a spouse travels frequently.

Some families pack cards or notes for the traveler to find while unpacking the suitcase. If the spouse is going to be at a specific place long enough, mailing cards really means a lot, too. Everyone loves to get personal mail, including the kids. Peter makes a point of mailing the children postcards if he is away for longer than a few days. It lets the children see Daddy is thinking of them.

Whatever method you choose to stay in touch, the goal is to keep the family a working and cohesive unit. The children need to know Daddy is readily accessible and that he cares about them. The continuity of parenting is possible and especially necessary when he is away. Sensitivity to your children's needs and emotions through making life simple, keeping a sense of humor, and predetermined disciplinary measures will help to allay their insecurities, resulting in a less stressful time of separation.

For Discussion

1. Discuss any recurrent disciplinary problems that occur when your spouse is away. Then work together on implementing solutions.
2. Write down three specific ways you can try to simplify your life the next time your spouse is away.
3. Relate a humorous story to one another from a previous time of separation.

4. Discuss and agree on "trigger" subjects to avoid while talking on the phone.

Family-Building Resources

For young children the book *Traveling Again, Dad?* by Michael Lorelli helps children, through the text and illustrations, to recognize their feelings when their father is away.

I like to cook, but I have found that simpler is better when Peter is away. Following are five quick, nutritious, and easy meals (and the kids even like them!) that have become standbys.

KIELBASA AND NOODLE CASSEROLE

1 package noodles or pasta
1 lb. fat-free polska kielbasa

Note: This recipe can be made with any semi-spicy meat or with no meat at all.

1 med. zucchini
2 c. spaghetti sauce
1 c. shredded mixed cheeses pizza topping
$1/4$ c. cream or milk

Cook your favorite pasta according to package directions. (For added nutrition use spinach fettuccine or vegetable noodles.)

Slice kielbasa and pan fry until slightly brown. Add sliced and quartered zucchini and cook with kielbasa for another three to four minutes.

Mix cheese into drained noodles. When cheese is mostly

melted, add spaghetti sauce and mix well. Stir in cream. Then add the cooked kielbasa and zucchini. Serve with a salad or raw cut-up carrots.

CHICKEN QUESADILLAS

4-8 flour tortillas (depending on appetites—
my children and I eat about one and a half
quesadillas, or three tortillas.)

2 c. cooked, seasoned cubed chicken

1 c. Monterey Jack cheese

For dipping:

1 c. salsa

1/2 c. sour cream

1 c. diced plum tomatoes

Place about 1/2 cup of chicken on a burrito. Sprinkle desired amount of cheese over chicken. Cover with another tortilla. Repeat for as many as desired.

Bake at 350 degrees for about ten minutes. Cut into pizza wedges and dip into above choices. Serve with a salad, refried beans, and nachos.

PITA POCKET PIZZAS

2-4 lg. pita pockets

1/2 c. pizza sauce or spaghetti sauce

1/4 tsp. basil

1/4 tsp. oregano

2 plum tomatoes, sliced
1/2 c. cooked cut-up meat (For variety use sliced turkey, bacon bits, chicken, i.e., leftovers!)
peppers, onions, mushrooms or
whatever toppings you like
1/2 c. pizza topping cheese

Spread pizza sauce on pita pocket to desired thickness. Arrange sliced tomatoes. Sprinkle basil and oregano over tomatoes. Add meat and any other toppings. Cover with cheese.

Bake at 350 degrees for about ten minutes or until cheese is bubbly. Serve with melon or grapes.

HAM STEAK WITH APPLES

1 lean ham steak (about 1 lb.), 3/4 to 1 inch thick
2 Cortland apples, cored and sliced
1/2 tsp. cinnamon
2 Tbs. brown sugar

Arrange steak in oven-proof dish. Cover ham with apple slices. Sprinkle with cinnamon. Crumble sugar over the apples.

Cover and bake at 350 degrees for about thirty minutes. Remove cover and bake an additional ten minutes. Serve with bread and string beans.

VEGETARIAN CHILI

2 cp. chopped spinach
1 16-oz. can stewed tomatoes with basil

16-oz. can red kidney beans
1/2 c. chopped celery
1/2 c. chopped green pepper
2 Tbs. minced onions
1/2 tsp. minced garlic
1-3 Tbs. chili powder

In large frying pan sprayed with cooking spray saute onions. When they are just turning brown, add garlic, celery, and green pepper. Salt and pepper to taste.

Stir in tomatoes and kidney beans. Cook for about ten minutes, stirring occasionally. Add spinach and chili powder.

Let simmer for at least one-half hour. The longer it cooks, the better it tastes! Serve with corn bread and salad.

9

Wholly Married: Building a Wall of Protection

WHAT DOES BEING WHOLLY MARRIED MEAN? IT MEANS IN everything you do, say, or feel, you take your marriage and spouse into consideration. Philippians 2:3-4: "Do nothing out of selfish ambition or vain conceit, but in humility consider others better than yourselves. Each of you should look not only to your own interests, but also to the interests of others." Try inserting your name and your spouse's name in the appropriate spots in these verses. It becomes very personal, doesn't it?

Being wholly married involves openness and giving of yourselves wholeheartedly to one another. The combination of honesty, integrity, vulnerability, purity, and selflessness melds the two of you as individuals into one. Two halves blended together to make one whole. Remember the marriage skyscraper or tower? Making a good marriage is a bit like mixing concrete. You combine sand with some accelerants and water. A chemical reaction occurs, and all the elements bond together to form an impenetrable barrier—rock solid.

This wholeness in marriage, however, is constantly challenged and under attack. Christians may encounter more temptations from

Satan because he especially wants to destroy Christian homes. He is the great destroyer and wants to chip apart your unity. The world says it is okay to divorce and even encourages extramarital affairs "if it feels right and you protect yourself." The media constantly run reports of the decline and demise of the traditional family. Talk shows honor dysfunctional people and families by putting them in the blinding limelight. This is all genuinely disconcerting and downright scary.

So you need to protect your marriage from the start, and then continue to preserve your family from direct invasions and sabotage. We call this "prepared protection."

Protection Begins Before the Trip

Unfortunately, the word *protection* has acquired some misleading connotations. According to today's morality (or lack of morality) protection means watching out for oneself by using a condom, taking a self-defense class, or carrying a gun. God's design of protection within the marriage bond means taking care of your spouse. He wants us to unselfishly nurture, care for, and shield one another from the rough edges of the world. We need to safeguard our marriages in everything we say and do—all the time.

This safeguarding cannot be left to the moment when your spouse steps out the door for a trip. If you haven't laid the groundwork together or prepared yourselves, you will not be adequately protected when your spouse ventures out from the fold of his family.

Josh McDowell, author, speaker, and head of Josh McDowell Ministries, has several self-protection policies when he travels. He always travels with at least one other male assistant. When he goes to a speaking engagement, he requires another male to pick them up at the airport. At his hotel he secures two interconnecting rooms for himself and his assistant to ensure he is never put in a situation where he could be taken advantage of, keeping him above reproach. These are the ways he and his ministry have chosen to provide prepared protection. Though few businessmen can travel exactly this way, the mind-set of protecting oneself can be emulated.

Know Your Spouse

Protection begins with understanding one another. Acknowledge each other's needs and concerns about the travel schedule. What routines does each person follow? How does your life with the children alter when your spouse is away? What does each of you wear, think, and eat when alone? Get inside each other's head and really understand what the other is thinking.

Some things I have learned about Peter are very interesting. He has a routine when he arrives at the airport. He buys a soda (or coffee if it's morning), gets at least one local paper plus a national paper, and then settles himself in the waiting area until his flight is called—simple, straightforward, and all Peter. When he arrives at his destination, he will only stay in hotels with remote-control televisions. He has been known to check out of a hotel within a matter of minutes if a remote isn't present. For his business appointments he always wears khaki pants and a blazer—never a suit. He likes to be remembered for his noncompliance with business protocol. He wants to be viewed as a hardworking man, not as a three-piece-suited, briefcase-carrying merchant. In sharing these little idiosyncrasies with me, he has allowed me to see him and know him in new ways. It is the nitty-gritty of who he is when he is away from me.

To have an understanding of what Peter is like when he is traveling also gives me a sense of remaining involved in his life. Besides being able to visualize him at business meetings or at the airport, I like to know where he is going to be and when. Likewise, he needs to know what we are doing in his absence. It keeps him grounded in his fatherhood when he is aware of the plans we have for each day.

Know One Another's Calendar

In the past I have become angry with Peter when he has not remembered what my agenda was for the day. If he knew (and remembered) my volunteer schedule on a Friday afternoon (which had been consistent for two years), why would he ask me during our evening phone call if I did anything special that day? I felt uncared for and basically forgotten. I was hurt. It was the out-of-sight-out-of-mind mentality. Because men are goal-oriented in nature, they sometimes move through life with blinders on, rarely seeing the peripheral unless they consciously choose to. The problem with Peter wasn't that he didn't care about us; it was that he was extremely busy, and if something wasn't written down, to him it didn't exist!

We came up with a solution that helps us to feel involved in one another's life, resulting in both of us feeling loved and cared about. Every couple of weeks we sit down with our individual daily planners and copy each other's schedule. Even using a different color pen can help to distinguish one set of plans from the other. Peter also types up a detailed itinerary of his flight plans and hotel phone numbers for me to post on the fridge while he is away. When he takes the time to do this, it shows me how much he cares.

The added advantage of knowing each other's schedule in

advance is the opportunity it provides to pray for one another. Occasionally, Peter has a big meeting with a potential new client. When I am aware of the meeting in advance, we have more time to pray about it together, and I'll know to pray at a specific time on the day of his engagement. Likewise, he can pray for me and the children when he knows we have a busy or taxing day planned.

Stay Spiritually Connected

Staying spiritually in tune with one another is another area of prepared protection. In your marriage building, the spiritual level is the base upon which everything else resides. If this aspect is ignored or eroding, the rest of the building cannot support its own weight.

We share and read the *Couples' Devotional Bible* every day at home. I always felt a little odd reading it alone when he was away—like a single person, an impostor, reading a book directed to couples. Peter came up with the idea of purchasing a second book for him to take with him when he travels. He reads the same passages I do, and we feel as if the Lord is teaching us and speaking to us about the same things at the same time.

Avoid Temptation

We probably all agree that sexual intimacy plays a significant role in the travel relationship. A man's sexual relationship with his wife is so important for his positive self-image, ego, and confidence that he truly can't function well at work without it. Most women desire sexual intimacy when they feel emotionally secure and loved. Once again, women are functioning primarily from an emotional level, and men are operating more from a physical level. That's how God designed us. And it is good.

Many sexual problems associated with the travel relationship are rooted in the woman's belief that she is about to be abandoned. Emotionally speaking, a woman can't possibly be intimate when her security is being threatened. Conversely, a man won't function at his best on his business trip if he is full of sexual tension. It boils down to the fact that he needs to make love to his wife before he leaves, and she has a difficult time accepting his need for her. A couple needs to discuss this issue and come to a compromise about sex before his departure.

For both of you sex is like the collateral for your time away from each other. It is the surety of your love and commitment to one another, expressed in a physical way, for you to treasure and remember in times of temptation. Sex sets you up for a positive and healthy time of separation.

Temptation abounds, particularly for the man, during times of business-related separation. He is surrounded by images (he is visually aware), words, gestures, and attitudes that may create problems for him. All his senses are assaulted by the world and its standards. Even his business meetings may compromise his ability to think and act "wholly married."

At the same time, his wife is at home possibly feeling uncared for, lonely, and vulnerable. She probably feels stressed and tired from a job, children, or demands of the home. She needs emotional support, and her main supply of help is absent.

These scenarios present a common danger: Both husband and wife are vulnerable to the seduction of another person. A kind word, a gentle, slightly flirtatious touch, or a listening ear all are potentially threatening to the unity of your marriage.

Beware of the Lonely

Several years ago an acquaintance of ours, Bill (not a Christian and not his real name), experienced the betrayal of his wife's leaving him for another man. We weren't surprised by the unraveling of his marriage, but we tried to be supportive and understanding of his emotions.

I tend to be a very compassionate and merciful person, with a history of an absorbing ear and a soggy shoulder. I'm easy to talk to, and I keep everything in confidence. Bill picked up on this attribute of mine and dove in headfirst, telling me all the problems of his past marriage. I became uncomfortable when he started calling every night. Then he began to "drop by" uninvited. When Peter was gone, Bill would call and talk for over an hour.

Peter began to feel uncomfortable, too, and asked me to stop "encouraging" him. I didn't feel I was acting inappropriately in any way, but I did sense that Bill had told me too much and that he saw our friendship in a completely different light than I did. The end came when he knocked on our door one night when Peter was away. I told him without opening the door that he could not come in. He was undoubtedly hurt, but I had begun to feel that my marriage was threatened. Bill wanted me to fill his emotional needs, and at the time I had been too concerned about his grief to see it.

We rarely spoke after that and then only in the presence of Peter. But it taught both Peter and me a valuable lesson. I had never been attracted to Bill in a physical way, but he interpreted my listening ear as something deeper than friendship. If I had hugged him, even once in compassion, what he might have thought or done makes me feel ill.

This scenario wasn't a tempting situation for me, but it could have been. If Peter and I weren't secure in our marriage and in our travel relationship, situations like this could happen routinely and end differently. Before Peter leaves on a trip, we try to persuade the odds to go in our favor. We talk about how to have "prepared protection" through prayer, understanding one another, knowing each other's schedules, and making love a day or two before he leaves.

Statements of Marriedness

Peter makes a pretty strong statement of marriedness when he is dining out on a business trip. He never goes into singles clubs or bars, even when he is with business associates. Once when he was in Atlanta at a convention, a group of business friends planned an outing to a strip joint. Peter absolutely refused to go. He would not compromise his marriage for the sake of a few business contacts.

Here's where the family pictures come in. Peter suggests putting a photo on top of the TV for a reason—to turn aside any thoughts of watching less than wholesome television. Face it, curiosity is the main factor that influences men to start viewing pornography. The combination of availability and privacy of porno movies in the hotel room sets men up for "just a quick peek."

I don't need to rehash the harm of pornography beyond saying that it is degrading to women and displeasing to God and that it encourages a warped sense of "normal" sexual relations. If the movie you glance at is something you would be ashamed to watch with your mother, then it's inappropriate and potentially dangerous to your marriage.

If the temptation is overwhelming, leave the room. Take a long walk, go work out in the hotel fitness center, walk around a mall, or have a snack. Remove yourself temporarily from the source of temptation. Then when you return to the hotel, don't even switch the TV on. Most hotels have the technology to "block-out" any channels you feel are undesirable. This was designed for families with young children, but it works for the wholly married businessperson, too. One businessman we know has the hotel remove the TV from his room entirely so there is no possibility of succumbing to temptation.

When Peter is traveling, he frequently eats his evening meal alone. This would be an ideal time for him to be struck with loneliness. Our social life revolves around food, and eating alone can be a desolate experience. It is logical and normal to desire companionship at mealtime. But Peter makes it very clear that he is not in the market for a dinner partner. He enjoys good food, well prepared, in nice restaurants. He also knows he could be a prime target for unwanted advances from single women who don't want to dine alone. His solution is to be really rude. No matter how nice the restaurant, he reads a newspaper while he is eating. Other times he will choose a family restaurant and watch moms and dads interacting with their kids. What he sees encourages him to think of us at home, keeping him in the family frame of mind.

Accountability

Sometimes the stress of frequent travel separations makes it difficult to be objective about the traveling itself, as well as about the other levels of the marriage relationship. It helps to have a friend who is sympathetic, either due to experience or to compassion, to whom you can talk to about anything. A friend of this sort will allow you to express whatever you are feeling, no matter what it is. Validation of the emotions an absent spouse triggers is necessary because it helps to dissipate any negativity.

In the sharing of feelings and concerns with a same-sex close friend, you have created a level of accountability beyond just your spouse. However, if you are dealing with numerous negative emotions or depression, it is extremely difficult to seek out friends. The time to nurture friendships is while your spouse is home. It does take a great deal of energy to invest in forming lasting friendships, but in the long run the return will help protect your well-being. These friends need to have the ability to listen, encourage, admonish when necessary, and be willing to pray with and for you.

My dear friend Beth is my accountability partner and reality preserver. Beth was home with four young children when her husband was traveling every week. Though her children are young adults now and her husband works out of their home, she knows and remembers the stress, fatigue, and yo-yo emotions that go along with a spouse's absence. I don't always call her when Peter is away, but I know I can count on her for emotional support anytime. She has listened and, with wisdom, advised me on every area of Peter's and my travel relationship. She has baby-sat my children when I needed a break, she has cooked dinner for us in her home if I was exhausted, she has told me to get a handle on myself when I've wallowed in self-pity, she has taught me how to be loving and welcoming to Peter when he comes home, and she has discipled me when I have felt far from the Lord.

Peter has formed a different kind of accountability support system. Since he owns his own company, he has instituted a men's prayer group that meets at his office early every Friday morning. The group, consisting of five men, briefly shares concerns and then prays for one another. The men may not have the same depth that Beth and I share, but they have a unique commitment to pray for one another, even if one or two participants are absent. This is so helpful to Peter, especially when he is away, because they continue to meet even when he isn't there. The other guys have even been known to pray in a car in the parking lot if Peter is out of town and has forgotten to leave a key!

Other forms of accountability groups are same-sex Bible studies, church-related women's groups, or Christian exercise classes. The important factors in creating or finding an accountability resource are that it be Christian and of the same sex. Because your spiritual life is the key to a successful travel relationship, the people that you choose to support you must be like-minded. They, too, must believe in preserving the sanctity of your marriage. It is important to have a same-sex accountability group or person. Vulnerability abounds in an accountability relationship, and this type of burden can only be shared with a man if you are a man and with a woman if you are a woman.

A mutual commitment from both of you to develop accountability support systems proves the depth of your pledge to one another and to your marriage.

Speak Positively

In Peter's business he sells a lot of pharmaceuticals to relief groups for third world countries. This aspect of his work is very worthwhile and gratifying. However, when people used to ask me what sort of work Peter did that required him to travel, I would say with a smirk that he was "a drug runner." I don't know why I thought it was funny. Probably because of the anger I felt about his traveling, I felt I needed to degrade him. Finally, I realized that what I was saying, even in jest, was compromising his character. My intent, subconsciously, was to make him appear corrupt and to humiliate him. Fortunately I've come a long way in my maturity.

Our policy now is the same age-old adage our moms and grandmothers taught us: "If you can't say something nice, don't say anything at all." 1 Thessalonians 5:11 also says, "Therefore encourage one another and build each other up. . . . " Peter and I take it a step further. We consciously say something nice about one another to whoever will listen. We build each other up when we are together and when we are apart. Peter is constantly telling his business associates how proud he is of my writing. I confidently tell friends about the type of work he does and how it touches people's lives all over the world.

When you build each other up, especially when you are apart, amazing things happen. For one, the person to whom you are speaking sees how committed and dedicated you are to your spouse and your marriage. What a terrific witness! Secondly, you begin to really believe and internalize what you are saying about your spouse. Proverbs 11:25: "He who refreshes others will himself be refreshed." Lastly, you will be more able to communicate these positive thoughts and feelings directly to your spouse, building his or her self-esteem.

The wall of protection and a wholehearted approach to your marriage will help to reduce outside threats. Through accountability and support groups or friends, you can gain listening and understanding ears, and supporters will encourage you in your marriage commitment. And the steadfastness of this commitment to one another will be evident in everything you say, do, and think.

For Discussion

1. Discuss how each other's routines change during business-related separations.
2. Talk about ways to stay spiritually connected.
3. Discuss situations that make you feel sexually vulnerable when you are apart.
4. Discuss each other's sexual needs and expectations in anticipation of a trip.
5. Talk about ways each of you can make "statements of marriedness."
6. Talk about who your accountability friends are or the possibility of forming a support group if you don't have one.

Family-Building Resources

You and/or your spouse may want to start a Bible study or support group using this book as a guide and reference. Following are some ideas to consider.

Discerning the Need

First, pray! Do you feel the Lord leading you and your spouse to host and co-lead this kind of support or study group? Avoid frustration and disappointment by waiting until you have a fairly certain yes from the Lord before investing any time into starting a group. Leave the rest up to the Lord—if He wants you to have this group, He will bring the right people at the right time!

Investigate within your church body or Christian community

to see if there is a need and desire for this type of study group. Contact other families you know who experience times of separation because of travel. It may take some initiative on your part to call vague acquaintances or friends of friends, but the rewards of a like-minded group struggling with the same issues as you and your family will be a valuable means of support.

Getting the Word Out

Phone calls to invite people personally are the most effective way to garner interest and advocacy for a group. You can also send notes with the dates, times, and meeting place as well as an outline or copy of this book for the interested people to review.

Discuss with your spouse whether the study should be a Sunday school class, a church-related Bible study, or a private group. Check with your church secretary about putting a notice in the bulletin. If church doesn't offer enough participants, you could also advertise in your local paper under community classes.

Group Dynamics

A group of four to six couples is ideal for open communication and allows for vulnerability after the group becomes comfortable with one another. It may take several months before the group is totally at ease with each other—even longer if all were total strangers at the beginning.

Make it an absolute policy that anything shared within the group is kept in complete confidence. Nothing will destroy trust faster than a blabbermouth.

Determine from the start how long the group will run. Most people don't want to make an indefinite time commitment, so it is better to predetermine that the study will last a certain number of weeks or months.

Naturally some members will be absent at times—most likely because they are away on a business trip! The spouse left at home may need help to make it to the meeting. As the leader, you need to do as much as you can to enable him or her to participate.

Always open and close the meeting in prayer—particularly asking for the Lord's direction on the subject to be covered. As the leaders, you are responsible to be sure the discussion stays on target by redirecting questions if someone is getting too far from the topic. There may be times when the discussion you planned can't be completely covered. Be flexible and finish it at the next meeting.

In most cases the couples you will be working with will have children and very busy lives. As common courtesy, always start and stop on time—leaving enough time at the end of every session for prayer requests and group intercession.

Using the Chapter Questions in a Group Setting

Depending on how many weeks or months you want the group to last, the book can be completed in a short twelve weeks (one chapter a week) for highly motivated couples, or it can last several months. We recommend dividing some of the longer chapters into two weeks, or longer if necessary. Of particular importance are the sessions on communication, expectations, and temptation.

The questions following each chapter can be used as group discussion questions, or the couples can answer them in private and bring their answers to the meeting for discussion. Be creative—think of your own questions, too. I don't believe I have thought of everything!

10

Taking Care

REMEMBER PAUL AND TRACY FROM CHAPTER 3—THE FINANCIALLY strapped couple? Their rocky beginning started nearly seventeen years ago with Paul's poor financial decisions. And even though they became Christians a few years after their initial vows, negative communication patterns from their preconversion days have lasted. Paul doesn't travel on business very often (sometimes Tracy wishes he did to allow them a reprieve from bickering). Their type of relational style, however, is too common. I call it the "uncared for = unloved" syndrome. Let me explain.

Paul, Tracy, and their two teenage children live in an old farmhouse in need of many repairs. Despite the "charm" of a historical home, Tracy hates living in a house where nothing is finished and nearly everything needs fixing. Whenever Paul starts a project, it always turns into a much bigger problem than he had anticipated. It seems that behind every wall he begins to repair is rotting wood, broken pipes, or frayed wiring. (Sounds a lot like some relationships, doesn't it?) Invariably he ends up over his head and completely frustrated. Tracy frequently and gently asks Paul to complete the projects, but he usually doesn't have the know-how, nor do they have the finances to hire a craftsman to finish the tasks. Consequently their interior decorating scheme includes partially plastered walls, exposed wiring, and rotting beams.

Most women feel that their house is a reflection of themselves. In Tracy's case this couldn't be further from the truth. She is an organized, attractive, well-manicured, and thoughtful person. She has lamented, hands waving at the disintegrating walls, "This isn't me!" She is embarrassed and ashamed of the state of her home and further frustrated by her lack of ability to change it. Because Paul can't fix the house, he turns a deaf ear and blind eye, ignoring the decay. Tracy feels that he is tuning out her and her feelings about the house, too. She thinks that if he doesn't care about her concern for their home, then he doesn't care about her as a person. And if he is unconcerned about her feelings, it follows, in her mind, that he doesn't love her. Consequently, uncared for = unloved.

Tracy feels emotionally abandoned. When women feel deserted, they feel uncared about and uncared for. Women (and men, too) need to feel taken care of and loved. If a wife is to have a continual feeling of being cared for while her spouse is away, her husband needs to have foresight and a plan to implement ways in which to care for her in his absence. This is the next step beyond staying in touch. It is anticipating in advance ways a man can care for his family.

Advance Planning

Think about the ways your spouse unconsciously cares for your family while at home. Talk about how he shows love and care on a weekly basis. Maybe he washes your car on Saturdays or takes out the garbage every week. Identify what he does that makes you feel loved, cared for, and protected.

Part of how Peter has shown care for me is by doing the grocery shopping. I have never enjoyed shopping, whereas Peter likes the hustle and bustle of a crowded store. When he takes the time to shop for me, it shows his love for me and how much he respects my feelings. Sometimes he even shops for me a day or two before he is scheduled for a trip, even though he won't be home to eat the food. His actions are very unselfish and thoughtful.

This advance planning is similar to what new moms and dads do after the birth of a new baby. Remember the first time you took little Joey out? I bet you agonized over what you could possibly need in the few hours you would be gone from home. Two changes of clothes, half-a-dozen diapers, diaper wipes, pacifiers, blankets, bottles (if bottle feeding), numerous breast pads if nursing . . . the list could go on. The point is that you both had the capability to think in advance and anticipate what you needed and what could go wrong. The same principle can be applied to a spouse's absence. Plan ahead for possible scenarios, because as any woman who experiences times alone at home can attest, it seems something always goes wrong when her husband is away.

Some other possible ways to care for your family is by ensuring that all the bills are paid, the car maintenance is up to date, the furnace is working, and cash is available. There is nothing worse than having a sick car when your spouse is away or a reminder call from the bank saying your mortgage payment is overdue. A working vehicle is sometimes the only avenue to sanity for a mother of small children at home without Dad, let alone for moms who work outside of their homes. A delayed mortgage payment threatens a woman's home and security. A woman will rightfully be angry about her husband's absence if one of these scenarios is endangering her mental well-being. She may be thinking, *He is supposed to take care of these things or at least be present to offer support!* Talking about possible problems—financial, car, children, or house—and then making a plan for dealing with any trying circumstances will help the spouse at home cope better should an issue arise, and will give a husband peace of mind from afar.

We have also found that compiling a list of "important people" to put on the fridge or keep next to the phone (Peter carries a copy of it, too) gives us both security. The list should be as comprehensive as possible, leaving out no one. In the confusion of an emergency, it's easy to forget phone numbers of friends and family, so leave nothing to chance and have all numbers clearly outlined for quick access.

During Peter's prolonged trip to Russia (really just two weeks—but it seemed prolonged), New England yielded to heavy winds and frigid temperatures. During that cold spell even cars kept in garages weren't starting. Peter knew it could be disastrously cold during his absence, so he made sure before he left that my car battery was fresh, there was gas in the tank, and windshield wash for the wipers. My car started faithfully every day. I suspect there was a little divine help here, but I still attribute part of my car's willingness to start to Peter and his care of us.

Taking Care of Mom

Taking care of your physical, emotional, and spiritual self is essential. The greatest threat to a mother's well-being, when she is going it alone, is her physical health. During your spouse's absence your body's defenses may be drawing on empty with fatigue and stress, increasing your risk of catching whatever virus is knocking at your door. Add to that possible hormonal factors, from premenstrual fluctuations to pregnancy-induced changes, and you may be in a physical as well as a psychological crisis. You need to take the extra precautions to replenish and maintain your health. Eating right and getting exercise and plenty of rest are the keys.

Some women don't know how to rest or take it easy. A friend of mine struggled with an upper respiratory cold that seemed to be hanging on for days. She felt worse and worse and finally began to run a low-grade fever. All her friends and family told her to rest, but she kept doing household chores, saying it wasn't stressful to maintain the house. Finally, after feeling weak, fatigued, and out of breath whenever she climbed stairs, she saw a doctor and was diagnosed with pneumonia. He put her on antibiotics and told her to rest, too. She confided in me a few days later that she honestly did not know how to rest. When she was sick as a child, the only rest she received was a respite from doing the dishes. My friend equated resting with laziness and needed to change her thought process before she could allow herself the chance to recover. Does this sound familiar?

Sometimes when a deceitful voice in my head tells me I don't deserve rest because I don't have enough check marks on my perpetual to-do list, I hear an inner whisper, "Be still and know that I am God" (Psalm 46:10). Be still, yes, motionless with no churning thoughts, restless energy, or drive to complete something.

The Lord nudged me into taking "stillness" to heart one time when Peter was away. He left on a Friday, and despite my usual reluctance to schedule a lot of outside activities during his absence, I had committed myself to hosting, co-hosting, or serving (I occasionally work for a caterer) at four different parties over three days' time.

By Tuesday morning I felt fragmented and tired. Thinking I would feel better if I could just work quietly at the computer for a couple of hours, I went into my office and switched the computer on. A sickening noise I have come to recognize as hard-drive failure came from the screen. My heart sank, and though it has happened a number of times (fortunately I always back-up everything I'm working on), it is still annoying. It meant a trip to the computer doctor half an hour away and postponed work on my project.

During the next four days while my computer was at the shop, every time I started to feel uptight about finishing writing projects, I seemed to hear a still voice say simply, "Be still and know that I am God." I felt the Lord telling me to actually lie down during the times I would normally be working at the computer. I complied.

Feeling more rested and less apprehensive than I had in months, I called for the status report on my computer on Friday. The man sounded a little confused. "Well," he said, "I've switched your computer on and off at least fifty times, and it boots up perfectly each time. I've checked all your systems, and everything is fine." Chagrined, I muttered my thanks and hung up. It occurred to me just how hard it must be for the Lord to capture my attention sometimes! He had to literally take away my computer to force my ears to hear Him telling me to rest. I've learned to listen more quickly and better now!

You can take advantage of the lesson I learned, too.

Actually sit down with your feet up—whether it is on the couch, in the tub, or in bed. If young ones at home still nap during the day, rest at the same time they do. If your preschoolers like public television or short videos, sit down and watch the show with them. If you work outside of your home, when you arrive home, sit in the recliner with your feet up for twenty minutes and read to your children. The important idea is to give yourself the time and permission to rest.

I became a firm believer and practitioner of naps a number of years ago. In college I found that if I napped between lunch and my midafternoon classes, my concentration was much better. One of the best ways of preserving physical health was passed down from my grandmother to my mother and then to me. We all take a nap, albeit brief, every afternoon. The Latin Americans have it right. A siesta clears the afternoon fuzzies and rejuvenates your body. Try it!

The other factor in keeping yourself healthy is to stay spiritually sound. Arm yourself daily with God's Word and time spent in prayer. Pray for strength, endurance, health, protection, and wisdom. "Therefore put on the full armor of God, so that when the day of evil comes, you may be able to stand your ground, and after you have done everything, to stand. Stand firm then, with the belt of truth buckled around your waist, with the breastplate of righteousness in place, and with your feet fitted with the readiness that comes from the gospel of peace. In addition to all this, take up the shield of faith, with which you can extinguish all the flaming arrows of the evil one. Take the helmet of salvation and the sword of the Spirit, which is the word of God" (Ephesians 6:13-17). Awesome assurance of God's provision and protection when we just pray for it!

Also, look for ways the Lord is providing for you and acknowledge them. I know that God helped my car start every day when Peter was in Russia. My water pipes froze only once during those cold days, and miraculously they defrosted with a hair dryer. And twice after returning home in the car, the snow on the hood had melted into the perfect image of an angel, wings stretched out in flight. I knew God was with me, and I thanked Him daily for His presence and intervention in my life.

But there may be times when you feel unable to talk coherently with the Lord because of stress or fatigue. You may not be able to formulate a prayer for yourself, but you can always ask the Holy Spirit to put your name in someone else's mind to pray for you or call someone and convey your prayer request. You may not hear how the Lord works in this fashion, but you will feel its effects. I remember one such time.

Jordan became very ill once when Peter was on a brief trip. I was exhausted from being up all night with him, and he didn't improve at all during the day. He was in agony with ear pain, and his temperature wouldn't drop below 102 degrees. The earliest appointment at the pediatrician's office was at four in the afternoon, so I picked up Geneva from school and dashed to the doctor's.

As I sat in the waiting room, tears pricked the back of my eyes. I was so tired and felt completely overwhelmed with my sick child. I closed my eyes and leaned my head against the wall. *Lord,* I said silently, *I can't pray. Please put my name on someone else's heart to pray for me.* Within two minutes an elder from my church walked into the pediatrician's office with his granddaughter perched on his hip. Our eyes met. He said simply, "Tough night?" I nodded. He nodded briefly back, said "Okay," went about his business at the desk, and then left. In that short exchange I knew that this man saw my need for prayer and responded to the Holy Spirit's nudging. I felt deeply grateful.

After seeing the doctor, Jordan took a dose of antibiotics and a painkiller and then slept for the next twelve hours. I had felt unable to pray for myself, but the Lord provided just the right person at the right time to intercede for me. I knew then that the Lord was my protector and provider always—particularly during Peter's absences.

I have also found when friends are aware of Peter's trips, they sometimes offer help or encouragement. If friends offer help, take them up on it. Even be bold enough to take it a step further and ask for help when you need it.

I remember one Sunday when Peter was away, I took the children to the early service at church because a special guest speaker was talking on the pro-life issue—a topic very near to my heart. As is sometimes the case, my children were less than angelic sitting in the back row with me. I became increasingly frustrated with trying to hear the preacher and contend with them. At one point I glanced behind me through the glass doors to the narthex. There stood several acquaintances who knew Peter was away. They were talking casually and looking in my direction, watching my children distracting me. Somehow in my twisted and irrational thinking I managed to blame the people in the narthex for my inability to hear the minister. My thought was if these "friends" knew I wanted to listen to the message, why didn't they offer to watch my children briefly?

In retrospect I see I was expecting them to read my mind. I'm sure if I had asked, they would have been happy to help me. Instead I left before the service was over, feeling uncared about and neglected.

The lesson I learned? Don't be afraid to ask for help. Be specific about how friends can help you with your home, children, or yourself. You deserve and need the assistance.

Taking Care of Dad

For men the attitude of taking care of oneself begins at home, especially when anticipating a business trip. Simply put, being sure you are well-rested and healthy will produce a less stressful trip. Sometimes men and women ignore their bodies' cues requesting rest. We overschedule, overcommit, and under-sleep. Men, in particular, need to pay more attention to their bodies and slow down the performance and achievement rat race.

You may need to take a look at how many outside commitments you have in relation to how much you travel. Church or community obligations just add to your time away from your family. Seriously pray about all commitments that would require you to be out in the evening or separated from your family. Too many outside activities will only dilute your energy level, leaving little resources to draw on for time spent with your family. If you travel twice a month, plus teach a Wednesday night Bible study and coach Little League on Saturdays, it may be too much. Are you sacrificing time with your family in the name of ministry? The bottom line is that your family needs you more than your church does—perhaps a hard dish of truth to swallow, but ministries must come after family. The Lord wants you to minister to your family's needs first.

John and Carol could easily fall into the trap of overcommitment. Carol's travel as a nutrition consultant and John's job as a physician require them both to be away from home frequently. Also, John is involved in various church ministries. Sometimes they both struggle with finding the proper balance between home and work.

They came to a compromise when Carol became the self-proclaimed "keeper of the calendar." Every month or so they sit down together with the family calendar, and John will inform her of his ministry commitments and work schedule. She adds in her own traveling, and then she "balances" the calendar by being sure they schedule equal time for them as a family. Frequently one or both of them must take a day or two off during the week. The great thing about their relationship is that John knows they need Carol to keep this balance, and competing time commitments are rarely a power struggle between them.

Just as a dad and husband can anticipate ways to care for his family during his absence, so can his wife think of ways to care for him on his trip. Discouragement may shadow his every move if he has had unfruitful business meetings and is feeling tired and lonely. These emotions are worse if the company is relying on the traveling businessman to "close the deal." He may be feeling a lot of pressure and needs positive reassurance from home.

Through phone calls, beeper messages, notes, or whatever way you choose, cheer and encourage your spouse. Ladies, your spouse needs to know he is your hero, no matter what. And, guys, if your wife is traveling, tell her she's terrific. Strong encouragement and validation while your spouse is on the road will help to bolster self-esteem and confidence and keep heartstrings tied to home.

A traveling businessman also needs to anticipate ways he can care for himself. Since most hotels have either workout rooms or swimming pools, take swimming trunks along or gym clothes. Exercise goes a long way to restore energy and help one keep a more positive outlook on life.

Illness can ruin a trip, and, as the saying goes, an ounce of prevention is worth a pound of cure. Consider getting a flu shot every year to prevent the worst illnesses. Most germs are spread hand to mouth—that is, your hands touch something contaminated with a virus or bacteria, and then you touch your face. Bingo—you're exposed! Washing your hands frequently and avoiding touching your face reduces the risk of virus transmission.

Carry a little medical kit in your briefcase with acetaminophen, adhesive bandages, heartburn tablets, etc. When Peter travels overseas, he carries with him any medications that could be hard to find in other countries—over-the-counter drugs for an upset stomach or diarrhea; ibuprofen for headaches, fever, or muscle pain; and decongestants for a cold.

Your physical well-being starts with what you put into your body. You know the saying, "You are what you eat." Ouch! Who wants to be deep-fried? Traveling business people very often eat quickly and alone when on a trip. Sometimes the quickest meal isn't the healthiest. And because eating tends to be a social activity, food becomes a friend and companion. The danger is obvious. Overeating, snacking out of loneliness, and eating simply for something to do all act to compromise your body's ability to function well. Because of the nature of Peter's business, sometimes he doesn't eat until the evening meal. He used to fast all day, then find himself ravenous at suppertime, and stuff himself. He'd overindulge and wake up with a heavy stomach and heartburn, which set him up for the same cycle all over again the next day. After too many lethargic mornings, Peter has learned to eat a small breakfast, snack on quick high-energy food during the day, and have a moderate dinner.

What, when, and how you eat will affect your levels of alertness and energy. Always eat breakfast (avoiding a high-fat menu), have a medium lunch (low in carbohydrates and high in protein), and then choose a moderate, nutritionally balanced supper. You will feel the difference in your increased ability to concentrate and will then be able to perform at your maximum.

Sometimes when you are away on a business trip or vacation, it's as if you are taking a break from real life and home routines. It is easy to minimize the necessity of daily time with the Lord. Because of this relaxation of home rituals, your spiritual health is at risk of sabotage. Having a hit-or-miss attitude toward your quiet time with the Lord is like playing Russian roulette with your soul. Sooner or later a loaded cartridge of sin will spin your way. Make a commitment to yourself, the Lord, your prayer partner, or accountability group to read the Word and pray every day of your trip. Even go so far as to write the promise down on paper, sign and date it, and carry it in your wallet. It will act as a gentle but effective reminder.

For Peter and me, reading the same devotional helps us to maintain our mutual growth in the Lord. Not surprisingly, when we are studying the same passages, the Lord convicts us simultaneously about struggles we may be having at home, or He opens the door for us to view a new truth about our relationship.

You can also take a portable tape player with headphones and listen to Christian tapes during long flights or while driving. The constant input of the Word will infiltrate your mind and help to keep the Lord in the forefront of your thinking. If you are gone from home over a weekend, look for a church service to attend. It doesn't need to be the same denomination as your home church; it can actually be fun to experience a different worship service. At the bare minimum watch a televised service on TV. Remember, your spiritual well-being is the foundation upon which everything else rests. Keep it strong with daily reinforcement.

A phrase from the Shakers, "Hands to work, hearts to God," reminds me that through our worship and submission to the Lord, we become more willing to use our hands to meet the needs of our families. This willingness, along with a determination to stay healthy in mind and body, will hoist your marriage above the status quo.

For Discussion

1. List and discuss three specific ways you care for your spouse when you are both home.
2. List and discuss three specific ways you can plan to care for your spouse during your next separation.
3. Talk about ways to give yourselves permission to listen to your own bodies.
4. Implement realistic ways you can stay spiritually connected when separated.

Family-Building Resources

Following is a suggested form for families to fill out, listing phone numbers of important people. This list can be updated as necessary—we suggest every six months.

A copy of this should be accessible next to the house phone as well as carried with the person who is traveling. Include on your list the following, plus any other important people you can think of.

All family members
Baby-sitters
Banks and account numbers
Both adults' and children's physicians
Car mechanic
Children's clubs and names of leaders

Children's school numbers and teachers' names
Children's friends
Church office
Electrician
Garbage collector
Handyman
Insurance agents
Neighbors
Pastor
Personal friends
Plumber
Police
Snow removal person
Veterinarian

11

Homeward Bound

THE MOVIE *PLANES, TRAINS AND AUTOMOBILES* IS A PERSUASIVE illustration of what a father will go through to get home to his family. If you haven't seen the flick, it's about a traveling businessman (Steve Martin) on a trip during Thanksgiving week. He plans on making it home the day before the holiday to see his daughter's school Thanksgiving pageant. Because of bad weather, his flights get canceled. He resorts to taking a train, calculating he can still make it home in time to see his daughter perform.

As the story unfolds, he winds up traveling with another man (John Candy), and they eventually must rent a car to make the last leg of the journey. Though the movie is a comedy full of mishaps, the desperation this man feels in attempting to make it home is real. He will do anything, try anything, to be with his little girl and his family for the holiday. Viewers, beware of the R rating because of profanity, but if you can overlook that aspect, the movie has a strong message and will probably make you laugh and cry.

A touch of desperation is often evident when a man or a woman returns from a trip. The possibility of delays or cancellations are as stressful as the travel itself. Dad is mentally returning to the family fold, and anything in his way had better watch out! He is a protective husband and parent ready to resume his roles, and obstacles will not deter him.

Numerous songs lament the emotions of men or women returning home. Simon and Garfunkel's "Homeward Bound" is probably the most riveting as it starts, "I'm sitting in the railway station, got a ticket for my destination. . . . " Then the chorus goes: "Homeward bound, I wish I was . . . homeward bound. Home, where my thoughts are creeping. Home, where my music's playing. Home, where my love lies waiting silently for me. . . . " The singers are so transparent in missing their home, their security, and their love that you can feel their vulnerability and wistfulness.

The parable of the prodigal son in Luke 15 tells of a son who takes his inheritance, travels to a distant country, squanders the money, and then realizes his father's household servants have more to eat and a better living situation than he has. He decides to return to his father regardless of the consequences. I can just imagine him, covered in the slime and filth of the pigsty, his arms hugging his knees tucked up to his chest, rocking himself and murmuring, "I just want to go home." Home—the place of love, warmth, acceptance, and security.

Prepare to Be Reunited and Reconnected

During his final hours before he returns home, a man will be thinking about his children and wife. He is subconsciously making the transition from his business role to his family role. He might be anticipating a happy reception and looking forward to family time. The problems arise when his expectations of his wife and children are different from theirs. Perhaps he pictures his children greeting him with hugs and his wife coming with open arms and a warm kiss. He may be in for a surprise if he arrives home to dirty dishes in the sink, toys littering the floor, and a grouchy wife. Depending on the children's ages, they may ignore him or hug him and say, "What did you buy me?" or run and hide from him. What a blow to his ego!

He needs a warm reception, and even if some leftover resentment lingers in his wife's attitude, she needs to try to have the home ready as a safe place for him to recoup. To a man home is where he can relax, be himself, and walk around in his underwear if he wishes. He needs to know he will be allowed to rest and rejuvenate before major decisions or responsibilities are cast at him. If the minute he walks through the door, his wife throws parenthood and other jobs at him, he can't possibly catch it all in one motion. Also, if he feels painfully hit with these responsibilities, he could perceive it as punishment for being away. He needs time to readjust to his roles as husband and father.

It is often said that a wife takes a house, a place of living, and makes it a home. Keep in mind that the traveler is fatigued and stressed from the trip. When he returns, he needs to feel he is home and rooted again. James Dobson's book *Love for a Lifetime* calls home "a place of tranquillity." Dobson's right. A man returning home from a trip needs to feel peace and calm when he walks in. The security and reassurance of his home, and sensitivity on the part of his spouse and children, will make his readjustment and transition time easier.

Years ago Peter expected banners, a cheering squad, and a very warm reception from myself upon returning home. It took a couple of years for us to discover that his expectations and what I felt was a loving welcome home were two completely opposite ideas. Because of his enthusiastic personality, he expected a high-energy greeting. And because of my subdued personality, I assumed he would be exhausted and just want to rest. After many disappointments, we finally learned that our differences influenced our homecoming expectations, and we began to alter our expectations. Now I attempt to have our home neat and tidy, the children in pleasant moods, and myself well-rested. The children offer him homemade cards. It is a good compromise for all of us.

As with all expectations in life, it is better to discuss them in advance than to live with the disappointment of unfulfilled needs or desires. Talk about what each person needs to hear or do when a spouse returns from a trip. Maybe the traveler needs to immediately go to bed and rest. Perhaps he or she wants to get right in with the toys and play with the children. The returning spouse may just want to sit and discuss the trip to "debrief" before being able to fully switch roles back to husband/father or wife/mother. The spouse at home may want to immediately give a rundown of the weeks' happenings or take a quick walk if he or she hasn't had any time away from the kids. Selflessly listening and discussing what each person wants and needs upon the return from a trip will help make the transition smoother.

The other area of homecoming expectations is sexual. A man has been faced with the blatant impurities of the world. He has maintained his marriage by not giving in to temptation. His wife also has been faced with vulnerability and has been successful in remaining committed to her marriage. Now they need to be together to reconfirm their love for one another. Sex is the ultimate reconnector. The problems arise when he or she may expect to make love before the spouse does. He may be exhausted and uninterested in sex for a couple of days. Or he may feel overwhelming desire for her the minute they are alone. Because a woman's sexual feelings are tied into her emotions, she may not feel able to express her love in a sexual way until she feels they have reconnected emotionally first.

The husband of a friend of mine traveled frequently for short periods of time. Every time he was scheduled to return from a trip, my friend would send her daughter to a neighbor's house, and then she would meet her husband in bed. The best way for this couple to gain access back into each other's life was to make love first. The talking happened afterwards. This scenario works well for them because they talked about it first. But it might not work well for other couples. You both need to talk about your sexual expectations before your spouse leaves.

It is also helpful, before the departure, to plan a nonsexual alone time together for when the person returns. This time can be used to talk at a deeper, more intimate level about what is going on in each other's lives. There are many thoughts and ideas that cannot be discussed over the phone or in front of the children. Concerns over a child's schooling, problems at work, financial decisions, and all the other details of marriage are ongoing, even though one spouse is away. It is necessary to plan time to reconnect to talk about these issues. After you both have had a few days of rest, go out to breakfast or lunch together. Or maybe put the children to bed early and have a late dinner at home. The perspective on any major decisions or concerns that came up during the spouse's absence will change and the urgency lessen when you are able to discuss them at length with one another.

Bringing Home Presents

Peter, being the generous person that he is, usually brings home gifts for at least the children and frequently for me as well. Though we appreciate his thoughtfulness, he has had to learn to moderate his giving because the children have come to expect a gift and are sometimes unclear as to whether they are looking forward more to Daddy getting home or to the present he'll bring.

Ben and Martha have worked out a moderate gift-giving method. If Ben sees something that reminds him of one of his children, he buys it. If not, he doesn't go looking for something to buy. And he never buys out of guilt.

The problem with buying due to the guilt of being away is that children may think that missing someone equals a gift. Though generosity is a good attribute to teach children, gifts should not be allowed to replace love or physical presence. Dad's presence is needed, not presents. Gifts can be thought of as a peace offering or apology. But there is no need to beg forgiveness through gifts when no wrongs have been done! Dad has been working, and he has remained faithful to his family and God. He has done nothing out of the ordinary except be physically absent from home.

For older children it is easier to explain a lack of gifts, but for younger children it may be more difficult, especially if they are used to numerous presents. Over time the habit can be broken however. Then Dad can be received back into the home without expectations or disappointments. Small gifts at infrequent intervals keep the giving in balance and prevent it from becoming a result of guilt.

Readjusting to Family Life

Because the nature of traveling perpetuates an attitude of self-centeredness, a spouse returning from a trip needs to consciously open back up to unselfish spousal and parenting roles. He or she needs to figuratively take off the business hat and put back on the family hat.

There may even be a rhythm, like the rise and fall of breathing, that offers comfort and security in knowing what to expect while a spouse travels. The cycle of being home, going away, being home again doesn't need to be vicious. It can be an ongoing circle of love and commitment for the family. The transitions can be confident and smooth because you both have talked through the emotions and issues you face when your spouse is away.

For Peter and me it takes a few days sometimes to readjust to our traditional family. Frequently after Peter returns from a trip, he must go right back to the office the next day, without much of a breather in between. It doesn't give us a lot of time to become reacquainted, but as I slowly warm to his presence, I formally reinvite him back into our lives. At this point I can mentally transfer the temporary sole responsibility for parenting and home back onto both of our shoulders. The relief from this heavy burden is welcome.

Neither Peter nor I sleep well when we are apart from one another. I miss his strong back to curl up against, and he misses my cold toes that willingly cool his warm toes. We both benefit with feelings of love and security from his return to our bed. The next morning or two after he returns, I feel a swell of warmth and assurance hearing him puttering in the kitchen making the coffee. I hear the patter of little feet as children rush to say, "Good morning,

Daddy!" When I finally slip out of bed, I feel truly thankful for his return home. I stumble into the kitchen, grab my cup of coffee, sit down at the table across from him, and say, "I missed you, and I'm glad you're home again."

For Discussion

1. Discuss what the word *home* means to you, and list three positive emotions it evokes.
2. Discuss and implement a gift-giving policy, including a budget.
3. Discuss what sort of homecoming reception you expect.
4. Discuss your sexual expectations for a spouse's return from a trip.

Family-Building Resources

Plan a surprise welcome-home party. It doesn't even have to have been a long trip or an overseas one. That's the element of surprise! Really catch your spouse completely off guard. If you are both social people, even go so far as to invite friends over to celebrate the return home. Make it a real party with streamers, cards of appreciation, cake, and ice cream. You'll make your spouse feel extra special and show how much the whole family missed him or her. And remember to take pictures to add to your spouse's traveling photo album!

12

Where Are You Going?

THE DECIDING FACTOR, THE CORE ISSUE IS: ARE THE TRAVEL separations you both endure worth the benefits you receive? I strongly believe that couples can work out an arrangement equitable to both sides—otherwise I wouldn't have written this book. Peter and I are a testament to the value of sticking it out and incorporating the travel relationship into the marriage, for the betterment of our partnership. We know that the trials and pitfalls of a traveling lifestyle have brought us into a deeper and more mature relationship with one another and with the Lord. We have taken James 1:2-4 to heart: "Consider it pure joy, my brothers, whenever you face trials of many kinds, because you know that the testing of your faith develops perseverance. Perseverance must finish its work so that you may be mature and complete, not lacking anything." The test of times apart is strengthening us, putting the finishing touches on our marriage, and making us whole together in Christ.

For you, only the two of you can decide if times of separation are going to benefit your marriage or detract from your long-term commitment to one another. You know what is best for you and your family. The issues that travel presents to your family may be different from ours. Our solutions may not work as well for you as they do for us. You may need to modify and make your own individualized plan for your family. But do make a plan. Try it for six months. If it doesn't work, alter it. In the long run you are making a decision about the job that requires the traveling—and possibly the career behind it. Each person's situation is so unique that only you can decide if traveling is worth the price paid for it.

Let me help you consider some thoughts and questions as you decide whether this lifestyle is hurting or enhancing your family.

Will Your Marriage Improve If Traveling Stops?

Take a long, hard look at this question. In what ways would your marriage improve? Why? How would your expectations of your spouse change if he or she were home more?

It might be easy to fall into believing that an end to travel will cure your marriage woes. As Peter likes to say, "If it isn't this issue you struggle with, it will be another." Having your spouse home and more accessible will open the door to other potential problems. I call them "replacement issues." There will always be a rebound result of whatever decision is made. If you fill a gap in your marriage building with a binding element, you can hear the hollow "chink" of a piece falling out of a wall behind your back. Now a new hole needs to be filled!

Look at it this way. Imagine if, after years of financial struggles, you suddenly had a financial windfall. All your money worries would be over, right? Wrong. The replacement issues would be how and where to spend it, save it, invest it, or give it away.

Undoubtedly, disagreements and fights would follow. Pandora's box revisited.

So it would be with the cessation of travel. A whole new set of problems would arise. Prepare yourself for that possibility and write down what exactly you both would hope to gain by eliminating travel separations from your marriage. You might be surprised by each other's answers. Maybe she envisions more house projects to tackle and complete. Maybe he eagerly thinks of joining a community sports team.

If Peter were to stop traveling right now, he would immediately sling his golf clubs over his shoulder and trot off to the local golf club to sign up for weekly tee times. But now, with traveling so much a part of our lives, he can't take the time to do that. He knows he is needed here at home. And he also knows there will be a right time in the future for him to be a part of the country club. He is content knowing he will join someday. It is a reward for him to look forward to when the traveling slows down and the children are grown. Maybe I can even join him.

What Sacrifices Will Be Made?

We are talking about changing jobs and possibly a career to remove traveling from your lives. Inevitably there will be changes. What are you willing to compromise on? Your income and standard of living? The town or state in which you live? Could it mean leaving family, friends, church, community, schools?

Beyond the physical changes to your living situation, what will it do to your self-esteem or your spouse's esteem? Could he or she feel manipulated or eventually resentful of leaving a secure job that happened to require travel, to enter an entirely new job or career? How could his or her self-perception change? Travel for business can be gratifying when the business meetings produce new clients, closed deals, or fresh orders. The businessperson's esteem and self-worth skyrockets. This boost might not be as easily replicated in the home office. Does the traveling person's personality thrive when doing business deals? Simply put, does he or she need the "highs" gained from traveling?

What Will Be Gained?

The saying goes that in the later years of life, businesspeople looking back at their early family years have never complained about spending too much time with their families. On the contrary, we hear over and over about men (and women) who wish, belatedly, they had spent more time with their children when the youngsters were growing up. This is time that cannot be replaced or regained.

At the end of 1995, the *Wall Street Journal* ran an article describing efforts of the new Congress that year to be "family friendly." The House had tried to take into consideration the needs of young families to spend time together. But by December three marriages of freshman members had broken up due to times apart, and at least three other Congressmen had decided not to seek reelection. Their families were suffering, and they felt they couldn't further jeopardize family stability for a political career.

As you climb the ladder of career advancement, are your steps ringing hollowly on the rungs? As you look down from your perch, is your family diminishing in size? Are family members feeling less important than your career? Are you sacrificing close relationships even as you reach for the next rung?

A move to a job that does not require travel would certainly open the door to more time for family interaction, bonding relationships, and church ministry. It would provide time to pursue new interests or further education. A whole new lifestyle would come into being. Is it tempting to turn away from the complications of travel to a simpler, steadier pace?

A good exercise for any family is to write out your family goals for the next year, five years, and ten years. Proverbs 29:18 says, "Where there is no revelation, the people cast off restraint." The King James version uses the word *vision* instead of *revelation*. I like that. The Lord wants us to have a plan, set goals (all mindful of and obedient to His will), and have a vision for our family lest we fall into the mediocrity of status quo. Think about your goals and talk about what it will take to reach them. Are they attainable only with more money? Are they "character-building" for the family? Do they revolve around deepening relationships with one another? Does business travel have an effect either way on reaching these goals? Making a long-term family plan can help you to make decisions now about your job and career.

Why It Works for Us

Simply put, it works for us because we want it to. We've weighed the possibilities; we've discussed the alternatives. There was a time when we seriously considered moving to Chicago to take over Peter's father's business. Much security would have come with this route had we chosen it—financial rewards, rare times of separation because of travel, excellent school options for our children, closer proximity to Peter's parents. All that notwithstanding, we opted to stay in New Hampshire. Why? In large part because we feel our travel separations are a gift from God for our growth. It's like He has given us an allowance, this gem of relationship options, that we can squander with resentfulness, anger, and jealousy, or that we can reinvest in one another, polishing our relationship. We've chosen the refinement process.

We also see travel as a blessing for Peter. Travel fulfills a deep need of his for excitement, a desire to see what's around the next corner, and to be a part of the bigger picture. His adventuresome personality would be stifled behind a desk. We both are comfortable with letting this drive of his be met "on the road."

Travel separations truly work for us, because the travel has forced us to be in constant productive communication with one another. Without travel interrupting our lives, I fear we would fall into a pattern of minimal interaction. Yes, travel separations force your marriage into what might be called a high-maintenance marriage, but who can complain about the positive outcome from hard work? For Peter and me, our stubborn commitment to going forward in this lifestyle has made us stronger. We honestly believe our relationship is more whole, more truthful, with a deeper commitment to one another, than it would be without separations in our lives. And we know this truth may be yours, too, for the taking.

For Discussion

1. Both of you write down the pros and cons of switching jobs to eliminate traveling.

2. Both of you write down what your expectations would be if your spouse were home more.
3. What are you willing to compromise on or sacrifice if a new job is sought? On what are you not willing to compromise?

Family-Building Resources

Make a family "life" plan and write it out on a calendar. Start with short term goals, things that require a minimum of time but that will build your relationships. Perhaps make a one-time commitment to serve an outreach ministry together—work in a soup kitchen or take part in a walk-a-thon for a Christian cause.

Write down a long-term plan, too. Maybe you want to hike part of the Appalachian Trail together before the children reach working age, or you want to visit the top ten museums in your state. At a family planning session, listen to what each person is interested in doing, write it down, and most importantly, set a date for it, even if it won't take place for two or three years. Having a firm date written in ink moves the plan from conjecture to reality, changing it from "wouldn't it be great someday" to "we are going to do . . . on such and such a date." Great things will happen in your family when you are working together toward a specific goal.